FROM I
TO LUCIFER...

Answers to Questions

FROM LIMESTONE TO LUCIFER...

Answers to Questions

RUDOLF STEINER

Twelve discussions with workers at the Goetheanum in Dornach between 17 February and 9 May 1923

English by A.R. Meuss, FIL, MTA

RUDOLF STEINER PRESS

Rudolf Steiner Press
Hillside House, The Square
Forest Row, RH18 5ES

www.rudolfsteinerpress.com

First published by Rudolf Steiner Press 1999
Reprinted 2014

Originally published in German (with an additional lecture dated 3
March 1923) under the title *Vom Leben des Menschen und der Erde, Über das
Wesen des Christentums* (volume 349 in the *Rudolf Steiner Gesamtausgabe* or
Collected Works) by Rudolf Steiner Verlag, Dornach. This authorized
translation is based on the 2nd, revised German edition edited by Paul
Gerhard Bellmann, and is published by kind permission of the Rudolf
Steiner Nachlassverwaltung, Dornach. The drawings in the text are by an
unknown artist and based on Rudolf Steiner's original blackboard
drawings

Translation © Rudolf Steiner Press 1999

A catalogue record for this book is available from the British Library

ISBN 978 1 85584 097 3

Cover by Andrew Morgan
Typeset by DP Photosetting, Aylesbury, Bucks.
Printed and bound by Berforts Ltd., Herts.

Contents

Main Contents of the Discussions

Dante wrote of the invisible world – the etheric world or world of spheres with the earth at the centre. Copernicus wrote of the physical world. Up to the end of the eighteenth century people still knew something of the etheric world. Phlogiston or 'fire stuff' theory, and Lavoisier's idea of oxygen. How materialism came about. First event after death is experience of complete recall. Dante's idea of hell.

4 *Discussion of 17 March 1923*
   The essential nature of man – life and death
   Comparing human and animal development. Walking, talking and thinking and the activities of ether body, astral body and I. People do not care much about the way they talk today. Most of them do not think at all; they are not able to take in ideas about higher worlds. Du Bois-Reymond's *Ignorabimus* speech. To die is to withdraw the ether body from the physical body. The ether body rapidly expands over the whole world after death. Pre-existence and post-existence. The Church taking responsibility for our dying. Life before birth and after death. We cannot know about life after death unless we also know about life before birth, that is, before conception.

5 *Discussion of 21 March 1923*
   Human life in sleep and death
   Importance of sleep and so-called sleeplessness. People sleep when they have gone out of sympathy with their bodies; they wake up when they have developed sympathy for the body again. After death we must rid ourselves of sympathy for the body; this takes a third of our life span. After death, human beings live a third of their earthly life span in the astral body, only a few days in the ether body. Ether body: second teeth. Astral body: sexual maturity. Once the astral body is laid aside, the human being lives only in the I. The rational mind, thoughts, are part of the universe; rationality is present everywhere. The wisdom that exists in the human body. How the human being comes into existence. Theory of evolution. Chaos when the ovum is fertilized. Man must create his own form. Everything that exists in the outside world is recreated in the human being. What the I must do in the time before the individual descends to earth again.

body easily unites with heat but not with cold; it is attracted by warmth. We are not yet human in our astral body on earth. Rabindranath Tagore's memoirs; everyone would beat him. Education by the rod. Slave natures and free natures. We take a moral impression of our life through death and into the world where we create our next life on earth. Every organ is supplied with nerves from two directions; it is, however, the astral body which intervenes. Everything that happens by way of movement in the human being is controlled by the astral body. Laying aside the inner astral configuration that has been gained in life. How we bring things we had in the previous life into our new human life. People differ because they bring different abilities and destinies with them from their previous life.

9 *Discussion of 18 April 1923*
Why do we not remember earlier lives on earth?
About Mehring's book on Lessing. Lessing's *Educating the Human Race*. Crookes and Newton. Primitive peoples all believed in repeated lives on earth. Effects of opium. Small amounts influence the ether body, the vitalizing principle, large amounts the astral body; habitual use of opium destroys the I. About learning to write and read. Conscious thinking and remembering. If one has taken up the right thoughts in the present life, one will remember the present life rightly in a later life on earth. Spectres. Spiritualist seances.

10 *Discussion of 21 April 1923*
Sleeping and waking—life after death—the Christ spirit—the two Jesus children
Venus's fly-trap. The concept of desire or appetite. The soul condition underlying the waking-up process; we wake up because we desire our physical body. After death the soul wants to get back into the body again and again; it is a habit it must get out of. Desire for the physical body and life altogether remains after death, and above all one has the desire to go on seeing all the things one has seen in life. The human being must lose the desire for the physical world before he can grow into the world of the spirit where he can perceive things in the spirit. England rising above and sinking below the sea. The relative position of the stars in the heavens sends

out forces to hold a land mass in a particular place. Plato about Solon. Julian's three suns. Baptism of John in the Jordan. Genealogies in Luke's and Matthew's Gospels do not agree. Details of two Jesus boys. Mr Hauer's views. World history took a different turn with the Christ event.

11 *Discussion of 7 May 1923*
On the Christ, Ahriman and Lucifer and their relationship to man
Man is not the same all the way through; he is always dying and coming alive again. Nervous system and blood system as opposite principles. Sclerosis. Growing old and growing young. Pleurisy or pneumonia—growing young is getting too powerful in us. If there were only ahrimanic powers we would harden all the time, turning into a corpse; we would grow pedantic, be philistines, waking up all the time. The luciferic powers soften us and make us young, make us dream and fantasize, going to sleep all the time. The human being needs both of these opposing powers but they must be in balance. Present-day education is wholly ahrimanic. Luciferic age from about 8000 BC to the turning-point of time, followed by an ahrimanic age. Pleurisy and birch charcoal. Stroke prevention with flower juices. Luciferic and ahrimanic diseases. The sculpture at the Goetheanum. About contradictory statements in the Gospels.

12 *Discussion of 9 May 1923*
The death, resurrection and ascension of the Christ
Early news of the Christians. The two Jesus children. Twelve-year-old Jesus in the temple. Kekulé's enlightenment. Thirty-year-old Jesus of Nazareth and his enlightenment through the Christ. Most important teaching in the ancient mysteries was knowledge of the sun. Death, entombment and resurrection of the Christ. Appearances of the risen Christ. Paul at Damascus. Ascension. The Pentecost idea—tongues of fire, a common religion for all. Earthly religions and sun Christianity.

Publisher's Foreword

The truly remarkable lectures — or, more accurately, question and answer sessions — contained in this book, form part of a series (published in eight volumes in the original German)* dating from August 1922 to September 1924. This series features talks given to people involved in various kinds of building work on Rudolf Steiner's architectural masterpieces, the first and second Goetheanums in Dornach, Switzerland. (The destruction by fire of the first Goetheanum necessitated the building of a replacement.) A vivid description of the different types of workers present, as well as the context and atmosphere of these talks, is given by a witness in the Appendix to the first volume of this English series, *From Elephants to Einstein* (1998).

The sessions arose out of explanatory tours of the Goetheanum which one of Steiner's pupils, Dr Roman Boos, had offered. When this came to an end, and the workers still wished to know more about the 'temple' they were involved with and the philosophy behind it, Dr Steiner agreed to take part in question and answer sessions himself. These took place during the working day, after the mid-morning break. Apart from the workmen, only a few other people were present: those working in the building office, and some of Steiner's closest colleagues. The subject-matter of the talks was chosen by the workers at the encouragement of Rudolf Steiner, who took their questions and usually gave immediate answers.

---

* 347–354 in the collected works of Rudolf Steiner, published by Rudolf Steiner Verlag, Dornach, Switzerland. For information on English translations, see the list on page xiv.

After Rudolf Steiner's death, some of the lectures – on the subject of bees – were published. However, as Marie Steiner writes in her original Preface to the German edition: 'Gradually more and more people felt a wish to study these lectures.' It was therefore decided to publish them in full. However, Marie Steiner's words about the nature of the lectures remain relevant to the present publication:

> They had, however, been intended for a particular group of people and Rudolf Steiner spoke off the cuff, in accord with the given situation and the mood of the workmen at the time. There was no intention to publish at the time. But the very way in which he spoke had a freshness and directness that one would not wish to destroy, taking away the special atmosphere that arose in the souls of those who asked the questions and him who gave the answers. It would be a pity to take away the special colour of it by pedantically rearranging the sentences. We are therefore taking the risk of leaving them as far as possible untouched. Perhaps it will not always be in the accustomed literary style, but on the other hand it has directness and vitality.

In this spirit, the translator has been asked also to preserve as much of the original style, or flavour, as possible. This might necessitate that readers study a passage again, trying to bring to mind the live situation in which the talks were given, before the whole can be fully appreciated.

S G

Rudolf Steiner's Lectures to Workers at the Goetheanum

GA (*Gesamtausgabe*) number

347 *The Human Being in Body, Soul and Spirit* (New York/ London: Anthroposophic Press/Rudolf Steiner Press 1989)

348 *Health and Illness*, vol. 1 (New York: Anthroposophic Press 1981) and *Health and Illness*, vol. 2 (New York: Anthroposophic Press 1983). Revised translation forthcoming, Rudolf Steiner Press

349 *From Limestone to Lucifer* (London: Rudolf Steiner Press 1999)

350 Four of the 16 lectures in the German edition are published in *Learning to See Into the Spiritual World* (New York: Anthroposophic Press 1990). Full edition forthcoming, Rudolf Steiner Press

351 Nine of the 15 lectures in the German edition are published in *Bees, Nine lectures on the Nature of Bees* (New York: Anthroposophic Press 1998)

352 *From Elephants to Einstein, Answers to Questions* (London: Rudolf Steiner Press 1998)

353 *From Beetroot to Buddhism, Answers to Questions* (London: Rudolf Steiner Press 1999)

354 *The Evolution of the Earth and Man and the Influence of the Stars* (New York/London: Anthroposophic Press/ Rudolf Steiner Press 1987)

The living earth — past and future. Natural healing powers

Questions were asked about colours and rocks.
Rudolf Steiner: Let me first of all deal with the question about rocks, for this fits in nicely with what we have been considering until now.

As you know, when you build something on this earth you must take proper account of the laws of gravity, of weight and many other things, and for instance something — we'll come to this in a minute — called the laws of elasticity. Imagine you are building a tower, let us say a tower like that of Cologne Cathedral, or you build something like the Eiffel Tower. You must of course always understand that you have to build in such a way that the thing does not topple over. Even the highest towers on earth are built in such a way that you have a base area, and if you take it up to about ten times this base area here, which would be one to ten, you can build the tallest towers. One to ten is therefore the ratio for building the tallest towers [Fig. 1]; otherwise they would fall over with the tremors which always occur because of the earth's movements, wind impact, and so on.

Care must also be taken to see that such towers have some degree of elasticity. The top always sways a little. Elasticity must be taken into account. The whole thing always sways a little, but not too much; if it started swaying too much it would break up. The Eiffel Tower sways quite a lot at the top. But care must always be taken not to go beyond the base area.

You'll find, however, that these laws are completely

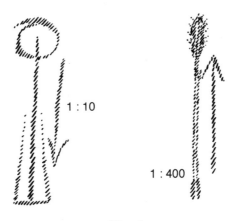

Fig. 1

disregarded when you look at a stalk of wheat, let us say. A stalk of wheat has a small base area. Yet it is also very much a tower. And such a stalk of wheat has a small base area and goes up a long way. If you calculate the ratio it is certainly not the 1:10 or so we have to stick to when building mechanical towers. It is 1:400, for example, and in some stalks 1:500 [Fig. 1]. Such a tower simply would have to fall down according to the laws engineers have to use on earth. When the wind sways it, its elasticity is certainly not of a kind that would allow you to understand this, using the laws engineers have to use. And if you wanted to put something especially heavy up on top of the Eiffel Tower, you'd find you simply cannot do it. But this tower, which is a stalk, has its ear at the top, rocking in the wind. You see, this goes against all building laws.

Now if you investigate the materials of which it is made, you have first of all wood. The material you find in your investigation is the lignin of which wood is made. Something else you'd find is bast, which you also know. You see it in trees. And then there is also silica, quartz in there, silicic acid which is a proper building material. It is hard quartz, as you find it in the Alps, for instance in granite or gneiss. This quartz creates a whole supporting structure. And the fourth material in there is water. And it is the mortar made of wood, bast, water and silica—this mortar makes the thing go against all earthly laws. A stalk of grass is therefore also a tower, built from such materials. It can be rocked by the wind and does not break in two, but calmly comes upright again when the wind has stopped or the weather is favourable. This is something you know.

But there are no forces on earth that would allow us to build such a thing using the materials of the earth. And if you ask where they come from, the answer has to be: 'The Eiffel Tower is dead, the stalk of wheat lives.' But its life does not come from the earth, its life comes from the whole cosmic environment. Gravity only exerts a downward pull on the Eiffel Tower, whereas a stalk does not grow by resting on what is below. Building the Eiffel Tower we must put one piece of material on top of the other, and this means that the lower part does indeed always support the upper part. This is not the case with a stalk. The stalk is drawn out into cosmic space. So if you visualize the earth [Fig. 2], and these are the stalks, they are pulled in all directions into cosmic space, for there everything is filled with a more subtle form of matter which is called the 'ether' and which lives in the plant. But this life does not come from the earth; it comes from cosmic space. And so we are able to say: 'Life comes from cosmic space.' And it is also because of this that—as I have told you once before—when an egg develops in the mother's body, the mother's body only provides the substance. The power that acts on the egg comes from the whole of cosmic space. This gives the egg life. The whole of cosmic space is the principle that acts on the egg. You see, that is how the whole of cosmic space acts in all that lives.

If you look at a plant, it first of all grows below ground.

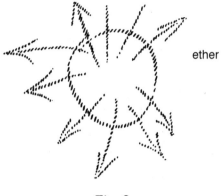

ether

Fig. 2

This would be the soil. The plant grows in there. But this soil is not indifferent matter; it is really something quite marvellous. In this soil are all kinds of substances. In earlier times three substances were particularly important in the soil. One is a substance called 'mica'. Today you find only little of it in a plant, but although only so little is found in the plant, it is extraordinarily important. You may perhaps recall, if you have ever seen flakes of mica, that it takes the form of small platelets, little platelets or flakes that are sometimes almost transparent. And at one time the soil was full of such mica flakes. They lay in this direction. When the earth was still soft, there were simply such forces. And other forces went across them; they went like this [Fig. 3], so that you had a real lattice structure in the soil. And these other forces are today found in quartz, in silica. And in between them is another substance, in the main, and that is clay. This clay connects the other two, filling in the lattice, as it were. As a mineral it is called feldspar. At one time the earth thus consisted mainly of these three minerals. But it was all soft, like porridge. There was mica, which really wanted to make the earth flaky, so that the soil would have been in horizontal flakes. There was silica in it, and that radiated like this [Fig. 3]. And the feldspar cemented them together.

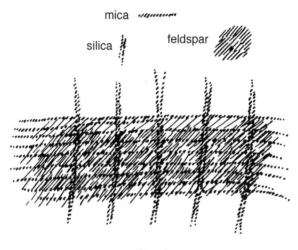

Fig. 3

Today we find these three main constituents of the soil if we take the clay that may be found in the fields everywhere. They were once mixed together in the soil. Today we find them out there in the mountains. If we take a piece of granite, it is quite granular. Lots of fragments are in it; these are split-up mica flakes. Then there are hard granules; that is the silica. And other granules link the two; that is the feldspar. These three substances have become worn down, made granular, and we find them out in the mountains today. They make up the ground mass of the hardest mountain ranges. Since the days when the earth was soft, therefore, they have crumbled, been broken down by all kinds of forces that are active in the earth; they have been mixed up, and today they are out there in the mountains, having worn down. But remnants of those old substances, above all remnants of the forces of those old substances may

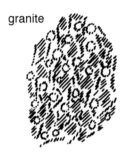

granite

Fig. 4

still be found everywhere in the soil. And plants are built from these remnants by the agency of cosmic space.

So we are able to say: 'Yes, these cosmic forces can no longer do anything today when they are active out there in the mountains. There the rocks have broken down, crumbled, become granular, and they are too hard to be made into plants. But when it comes to what is present in the soil, this can still be used to build up the plant out of cosmic space — above all because the soil still gives the seed its most important substances and forces.'

You see, gentlemen, looking at things like this, taking into account that the whole of cosmic space plays a role in making things live — such an approach does not exist in modern science. The other day — you may have read about it — a talk was given in Basel[1] about how life is supposed to have come to the earth, and the speaker said: 'Yes, it is hard to imagine that life comes into existence merely by the mixing or chemical interaction of substances on this earth; and so it must after all come from cosmic space. But how?' Well, it is interesting to hear that a modern scientist thinks life may come from cosmic space. He said to himself: 'Well, if it is not on earth it must come from other stars.' Now, the nearest star that may perhaps at some time have shed some substances which would then have flown down to the earth is so far away from the earth that those substances which have been shaken off there would have needed 40,000 years to fly all the way to the earth. One would therefore have to think, people say to themselves, that the earth once was fiery and liquid, a fiery body. Life would not have been able to exist on it, for it would, of course, have burned to death. But the earth has cooled down. Once it had cooled down it would have been in a condition where it could have received any life that might have flown to it from the nearest star from which people think it might have come, taking about 40,000 years to fly all the way.

It is impossible to imagine, the speaker said, that a seed of life, a small seed of life, moved through cosmic space for 40,000 years, a space, what is more, that is cold, not warm, the temperature being minus 273 degrees centigrade. The seed would then arrive on earth and life would arise on earth. Before, all seeds, however many might have arrived, would have been burned. But once the earth had cooled down sufficiently, they would have developed. But, the speaker said, that simply could not be. And so people do not know where life comes from.

But we can see that it comes from cosmic space. We can really see that anything that lives has more than earthly forces active in it. For we use the forces of the earth to build the Eiffel Tower, for instance. And in a tower like this [Fig. 1, wheat stalk] it is not only the forces of the earth that are active, but forces from the whole of cosmic space. And when the earth was still soft, when mica, feldspar and silica were still mingling in it as fluids, the whole earth was under the influence of cosmic space. It was then one vast plant. So if you walk in the mountains today and find granite there or gneiss — which only differs from granite in that it has more mica, which is more in evidence — these rocks are residues of ancient plant material. The whole earth was a plant. And just as when a plant dies today its mineral constituents become part of the earth, so the whole earth body later gave its mineral constituents – from when it was still a plant – to the earth. And so you have the mountains today. We are therefore able to say that the hardest mountains that have developed, these hardest mountains have arisen from plant nature, and the whole earth was a kind of plant.

I did tell you[2] what things were like on earth when this rock material had just stopped being plant but everything was still soft. Our present-day animals and human beings did not exist then, but the megatheria[3] and all the kinds of animals about which I told you before. But before all that happened, the earth was a giant plant in cosmic space. And if you take a plant today and enlarge it in your mind you will still find that parts of it look very similar to the mountain ranges outside. This is because the life that comes from cosmic space acts on the whole plant. Small parts of it are already rock masses. But the earth did once live, and we find a remnant of what once was living earth in the hardest mountain rocks.

But the hard material, the earth's rock material also arises in another way. When you go out to the ocean you find islands. So that would be the sea [drawing]. Some distance below the surface small creatures live in real colonies – coral. The special thing about corals is that they continually secrete chalky matter. This chalky material remains where it is, so that the island is covered with limestone deposits that come from corals. And sometimes a depression will form here, with the ground going down, and a lake develops. You then have a ring of limestone left behind by the corals. It is altogether the case that the ground is continually sinking in the regions where corals secrete chalky material, so that the chalky material produced by them – and they can only live in the sea itself – goes down lower and lower. We may say, therefore, that we still find lime deposits in the sea today that come from creatures, from the corals. In the past, animals existed in the places where the Jura limestone is now.[4] They deposited the limestone.

If you go to the middle part of the Alps where the hard rocks are, you have material deposited by plants. If you go into the Jura mountains here, you have material deposited by animals. The whole earth has once been alive. Originally it was a plant, then an animal. The rock materials we have today are leftovers of life.

It is simply nonsense to say that life develops from chemical compounds made of dead matter. Life comes from cosmic space, and this is filled with ether. It is nonsense to say that dead matter can get mixed together and come alive in a process called 'spontaneous generation'. No, dead matter always comes from something that was alive; it has been secreted by life forms. Just as our bones have been secreted — we do not have them in the womb to start with — so everything by way of bone development and so on arises from the sphere of life. Life is there first, and dead matter only comes later. It is such that the ether is all around us, and the ether pulls everything upwards just as earth's gravity pulls everything down. But it does not make things dead in pulling them upwards, which is what gravity does. The more you breathe in gravity the more you will be gouty, diabetic or the like; the more we come to be dead. And the more the powers that move in an upward direction come into play in us, the more alive shall we be.

You see, I now come to a part of the question put by Mr Burle. Imagine therefore I have a person before me who is sick in some way and I can say to myself: 'The problem with him is that he has too few forces that act out into cosmic space. He has too much of the forces of gravity. All kinds of things are getting deposited in him.' Then I remember: 'Wow, silica has once been something that made forces radiate out into cosmic space. If I prepare silica in such a way that the old powers come alive again in it, that is, if I make a medicine of silica, adding other substances, so that the silica regains its old ether powers – if I give that to the person, I can make him well.' And one can get very good results with this silica medicine. We are thus able to use the forces which silica once had when it was in the sphere of life, and we can altogether get very good results in medicine if we think a little about how things were with the earth when it was still wholly alive, when the silica was still under the influence of cosmic space. So if there is not enough life in a person and he needs to be connected with cosmic space, we give him substances that lie out there, having hardened, substances that make very good medicines.

The head goes out furthest towards cosmic space. It can therefore be healed most easily with silica. The belly comes closest to the earth, and we therefore can most easily heal it with mica. And the parts that are more in the middle, the lung and so on, can be treated to good effect with feldspar, if we prepare it in a suitable way.

So you see that if we understand nature we do indeed also understand the principles that are powers of healing in human nature. But we have to have a feeling for it that cosmic space is actively involved in our earth.

You see, it is always only possible to explain particular things at particular points. Thus I can now explain the migration of birds to you from a different point of view than I did some time ago, when we had not yet got so far. Modern scientists take a highly abstract view of the migration of birds in autumn and spring. In spring the birds leave the warmer climates where they then are, and in the autumn, when it gets colder, they leave the regions that are more to the north. But there are also birds that cross the ocean. And it is quite strange; these birds fly very fast and do not stop to rest. It is possible to prove this for there are no islands along some of the routes such birds will take. People do not discover how these birds get their sense of direction. People have said: 'Ah well, it's an inherited characteristic; the young birds have always inherited it from the old, and the old birds will instruct the young ones, and then it works quite well and the young birds can also do it.' When autumn comes, therefore, the old swallows set up a school; the young are instructed. The old birds then fly off, with the young ones following, doing the same. That is how people thought it went. But not all migratory birds do this. This is very strange. It is often the case among migratory birds, in Africa, for instance, that the old birds fly off first to return to us. The young birds manage to stay longer in Africa, for they are still strong. The old ones depart earlier, leaving the young ones behind. They do not instruct them, nor do they act as guides. The young birds have to find their way entirely by themselves.

Some people have said: 'Ah well, birds are able to see a long way.' They would therefore need to be able to see what's going on over there in Africa, and perhaps even see through the earth! We don't get very far in this way. But let me give you an example from which you can see how things really are. There is something else where we may marvel at the way things go—and that is a ship. How does a ship find its way when it is supposed to go from Europe to America? It takes its orientation from a compass. When people did not yet have compasses ships had a difficult time. They had to follow the stars. They now follow the compass, that is, invisible forces that exist in the ether. These are also the forces from which birds take their direction. Birds have a sense for this; they have an internal compass. We ourselves have to make some effort and first learn how to use a compass, a magnetic needle, to see the ether forces. A bird has this by nature. It follows the ether, something that is active in cosmic space.

And so we are able to say: 'The earth is surrounded by

ether. The ether contains the powers of life. These come from cosmic space, take the physical matter of the earth and make living things out of them.'

But something always remains in there as a residue of life. If you take coral limestone, for example, there is always still something in it at the beginning that reminds us a little bit of life, something that has been taken from life. Because of this you can still discover all kinds of things in there which if added to life can be good medicines. And if, as I said, you take silica, which has by now become extremely hard, and add it to human life, you can above all treat illnesses in the head very nicely with it.

So the life principle is still in there. The whole was once alive. We cannot say that the rocks are still alive today, but they did once live. They were parts of life once. And a residue has remained in them which we can draw out from them by all kinds of means, and because of this residue they serve well as medicines.

So that is the answer to the question as to whether there's still life in stones. Someone who reckons only with the forces that are active on earth today will be able to say: 'Things looked different on earth millions of years ago.' But he's not taking account of heavenly space. As I told you the other day, if we take account of the things that come from heavenly space, we do not arrive at such vast numbers of years, but we discover that here in our parts everything was still frozen ice at a time when over there in Asia people already had a very great civilization—much wisdom then lived among human beings. But we altogether come to realize that our earthly life is in a way dependent on the life out there in cosmic space. And we may say that we need only go back six, seven or eight thousand years and the earth was completely different in its rocks than it is today, not so much on the outside, but inside. And we then move further and further back until we come to the earth in its soft state.

If we want to take note of cosmic space, we must also observe cosmic space in the right way. Now one way of observing cosmic space is to observe the sunrise in spring. Today the sun rises on the morning of 21 March at a point where it has the constellation of the Fishes behind it. But if we go further back through history, for instance to the time before Christ was born, then the sun did not rise in the constellation of the Fishes but in the constellation of the Ram. If we make a drawing [Fig. 5] it is like this. If the sun rises in the Fishes in spring, on 21 March, nowadays, it rose in the Ram about 2160 years ago, and earlier than that in the Bull, and even earlier in the Twins. There are twelve such constellations. The point where the sun rises is always moving on, going all the way round the circle. The spring equinox thus goes right around the cosmos. It keeps moving from west to east.

You see, there we discover that at an earlier time the sun rose in the Ram, before that in the Bull, before that in the

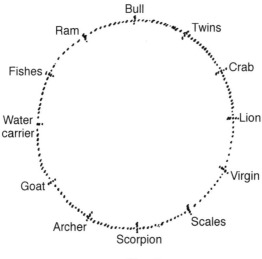

Fig. 5

Twins; then in the Crab, the Lion, the Virgin, the Scales, Scorpion, Archer, Goat, Water Carrier and today in the Fishes. So if we go back 2160 years, it rose in the Ram, another 2160 years earlier it rose in the Bull, yet another 2160 years earlier in the Twins, another 2160 years earlier in Cancer. Then we come all the way round, and at one time it rose in the Fishes. We get all the way round [drawing]. The sun moves in a circle. In 25,920 years it goes right round the whole world.

This is very interesting. And from this movement of the heavenly bodies we can see how everything on earth changes. You see, gentlemen, under the conditions under which the sun rises today we have high mountain ranges with dead masses of granite, containing feldspar, quartz and mica. There everything has dried up, turned to arid waste. That's also how it was 25,920 years ago. At that time things were similar on earth. But not in between. In between the sun will have been in the Scales in spring, for instance, at one time, between the Virgin and the Scorpion. Then everything was full of life, the whole was soft and the earth was a kind of plant. We need not go back more than 15,000 years at most, and then the whole earth was in plant form, because the sun's position was very different, and later on in animal form. And from this influence that comes from cosmic space, and which we can follow by observing the sun, we can see how the earth has changed.

Going back, therefore, you have to think of the rocks, which are utterly solid in the original Alps, beginning to flow, more or less the way iron flows in foundries. That is, it is not entirely that way, but if we go back the flowing is the other way round at first, a process of solidification. But if we now go forward into the future, we'll have the sun in the Scales again some time. Now it rises in the Fishes, 2160 years later it will be in the Water Carrier, then in the Goat, the Archer, the Scorpion and once again the Scales. And when the sun will be rising in the Scales again at a future time, then all the original Alps will have dissolved. The dense quartzes will have become watery again, and the earth will be a plant again, with human beings and animals returning to the states in which they have been at an earlier time. In the meantime, however, they will have taken up into themselves everything they have been able to take into themselves on this earth.

And so everything really goes in cycles. We look back, therefore, to an earlier time where the earth was fluid in what are now its hardest forms. Then the matter that was on top was such that it produced the animals which I have described to you before, animals that came into being under the influence of the heavenly forces and then died. Then everything cooled down. Solid forms arose, and gradually life came to be as we know it today. But this will change back again. The granular quartz and granite and so on will dissolve, and a state of life will exist again, only at a higher level of evolution.

If you pick up a piece of granite today, which has quartz in it, you can say to yourself: 'In this piece of granite, which has quartz in it, I can also see something that will live again in future. It has lived before. Today it is dead. It has created solid ground for us to walk on. When we did not yet need to walk, the solid ground did not exist. But it will live again.'

We may really say that the earth merely sleeps in relation to the cosmos; only it is a long sleep, 15,000 years at the least. Once it lived. Then it was awake, was connected with the whole of cosmic space. The cosmos then used its powers of life to put those large animals on it. Later, when solid matter developed, it put human beings on it. Now human beings have it good on earth — this is with reference to the cosmos, of course, not to the earth itself. You are able to walk on the solid ground. But this solid ground will wake up again — it is really only sleeping — it will wake up again and be living life. When we take a piece of limestone today, just an ordinary piece of limestone from the Jura, we have to say it is the residue of a piece of life. It has been secreted out from life, but will live again; it is between life and life, really only sleeping.

Now we can use limestone very well if we make it into a medicine,[5] for instance if we find that children, let us say, cannot take nourishment properly. That can be seen especially in Germany at present. It is quite terrible in Germany at present. The other day, when I got to Stuttgart and inspected the Waldorf School again, I was in class 1, for example. It has 27 children but only nine were there; the others were all sick. Fifteen were sick in another class. And if you follow this up you discover terrible things. They brought a small boy to me in the conference room, for instance, and said: 'What are we to do with him? The doctor has already given him up. He can't eat any more.' Of course, with malnutrition the digestive organs gradually get in the habit of not digesting anything at all any more, they reject everything. People are no longer able to eat, however much you give them. You can have food donated by the Quakers and do all kinds of things—they will not help this child at this time, because his organs are no longer working. He looked rather bloated. What should one do in such a case? One must first make the organs fit again to be able to take in food.

This is where the little bit of life in the limestone serves us well. If the limestone, or calcium carbonate, is used as a medicine in the right way, we can wake those sleeping digestive powers up again and the child will live. And the child should then be given such a quantity of this calcium carbonate, but together with other substances, for it does not act on its own. It needs to be such that it can really enter into the organism—just as we have to cook foods together with other substances. The calcium carbonate will still be taken up if it is given to the child in a 5% concentration, let us say.

But what are we using when we give that 5% of calcium carbonate? We are using powers that in earlier times were powers of life in the limestone. These are still in there. We use them to vitalize the matter. But if one reduces the calcium carbonate and makes it very fine, a 'homoeopathic dose', as people say, so that it is not 5% but 5:10,000, not even just 1,000 but 10,000, and one is adding the calcium carbonate to other substances in this 'homoeopathic dose', which is very small, then the limestone acts on the head; it suddenly becomes a medicine for the head. Given in allopathic doses,[6] it acts on the digestive organs; given in very high dilution it acts on the head. And we can arrange things accordingly. But we can also know what we are using when we give calcium carbonate in very high dilution. We are using powers of the future. These are still in there and will be active again in the future.

You see, that is how one must know the natural world. Then it is possible to make medicines of it, for there has been life everywhere and there will be life again, with death only an interval between two lives. The right way can be found to use the powers of life from the past in the rock, and the powers of the future.

You also see the following from this. Looking out into the world today, you have allopaths and homoeopaths. The allopaths use allopathy to treat diseases, the homoeopaths homoeopathy. Well, gentlemen, it is not possible to cure all illnesses homoeopathically. Some have to be treated allopathically. For this, the medicines must be made up in a different way. It means we should not be fanatics, swearing by words, but prescribe medicines on the basis of real and complete knowledge, sometimes one way, sometimes the other. This is so in the case of anthroposophy, for here we do not go by slogans but consider the matter at hand, saying

'The allopath addresses himself above all to the stomach, intestines, kidneys; there he gets his results. The homoeopath gives effective treatment if the sicknesses have their point of origin in the head, as in the case of influenza. Many sicknesses have their origin in the head.' So we need to know how things really work in nature. Today people no longer know anything and therefore produce slogans. These are always produced when people no longer understand things. The truth is, of course, difficult to find in that case, for the allopath will say, 'I have cured people so and so many times,' and the homoeopath will say, 'I have cured people so and so many times.' They do of course always omit those they have failed to cure.

But you see, even a physician and professor who can in no way be accused of not knowing everything about modern medicine — that was professor Virchow in Berlin,[7] even the freethinkers said he was a true liberal — but with regard to curing diseases he had to admit the following: 'When a physician in modern medicine is able to say he has cured 100 people, it really has to be said that 50 of those 100 would also have got well without him, and 20% would have got well even if he had given them completely different medicines; 70% are thus not cured by modern medicine but only 30% at the most.' Those are the calculations made by Virchow, who knew all about modern medicine.

Well, gentlemen, we simply have to say that the right medicine, used in the right way, does have an effect. Everyone can find out for himself the truth about syphilis as I presented it to you.[8] Treatment with mercury is effective, though it does have side-effects, harmful side-effects. And so one must find the right thing to do. Sometimes it is terribly complicated. Sometimes the organism has grown so fragile that it cannot cope with the cure. But in a certain sense one can see, if one has genuine knowledge of what exists in nature, how individual substances act on human beings, for being dead matter they are half-way between two lives. But one must, of course, know the life of those substances.

Well, gentlemen, the strange thing is that to understand something you must always start from life. And so we must also start from life to understand colours.

You see, when you look at paintings today, they are painted on. But you sometimes have the feeling that there is no flesh behind the image, only wood that has been given a coat of paint. Modern painters do not manage to produce a flesh tint, or incarnation, because it also does not live in their feelings. The flesh tint is produced out of the human being. It does not appear in any other form of matter. But you have to understand the flesh tint, and then you can understand the other colours. I'll therefore speak about this the next time.

The child who was brought to me and who is being treated with a calcium carbonate preparation — I hope we'll manage to save him and that the situation does not arise where people may say: 'They did not use a proper medicine … [gap in text].' He had completely lost his flesh tint, had turned yellow from inside. The living reality is part and parcel of the colour. And because of this we have also made the attempt to use less dead material for our colours. We have been using vegetable colours to paint the walls and ceilings in the Goetheanum, for they come more from the sphere of life. So you see, with colours, too, we must go for the sphere of life.

I'll tell you more about this next Wednesday.

You see, the question if stones have life was not that stupid. It is perfectly sensible, for it has given us the opportunity to discuss how stones live during a period when the earth is alive, and then die again, and so on, and how life relates to this.

The two basic principles of colour theory in red sky at dawn and dusk and blue of the sky. Sickness and health in relation to colours

To answer your last question properly, I'll say a few things about colours after all, to the best of my ability.[9]

We do not really understand colours unless we understand the human eye, for people are only conscious of perceiving colours with their eyes. They know nothing about the way they perceive colours in other ways, though they do in fact perceive them not only with their eyes. Imagine a blind person, for example. He'll feel different in a room that is illuminated than in a room that is dark. This is so slight, however, that he'll not be aware of it. It is such a slight thing. It is actually very important for him, but he is not aware of it. Even a blind person could not live permanently in a cellar, for instance. He does need the light. And there is a difference if you put a blind person into a brightly lit room with yellow windows, for example, or into a dark room, or, if you like, a less dark room that has blue windows. This has a very different effect on life. Yellow and blue have a very different effect on life. But we only come to understand such things when we have grasped how the eye relates to colour.

From what I have told you on other days, you will perhaps have seen that two things are most important to the human being. Two things are most important in the whole of his organism. The first of these is the blood. For if human beings had no blood they would have to die immediately. They would not be able to renew their life moment by moment, and life has to be renewed moment by moment. So if you think of a body without blood, the human being is a dead object. But also if you think the nerves away. The person might look exactly the way he does now, but he would have no conscious awareness; he would not be able to have ideas, to feel, would not be able to move. So we must say to ourselves that man needs nerves if he is to have conscious awareness. He needs blood to be able to live at all. The blood is therefore the organ of life; the nerves are the organs of the conscious mind.

Every organ has both nerves and blood, however. Basically the human eye is really a whole human being, with nerves and blood. It is like this — if you think of this as the place where the eye emerges from the head [Fig. 6], there are small blood vessels present everywhere in it. Many small blood vessels spread out there. And many nerves also spread there. So you see, you have nerves and blood flow in your hand and also in your head. The situation in the eye is like this. Just think, the outside world, which is illuminated, acts on the eye. You see, you find it easiest to get an idea of the outside world when it is illuminated. And during the day the outside world in which you walk about is illuminated. But it is difficult to get an idea of this whole illuminated outside world. You get a true idea of it if you

Fig. 6

visualize it in the morning or evening half light, when you see the red dawn or dusk all around you. The red dawn or dusk are particularly instructive.

What exactly are the red dawn or dusk? Think of a sunrise [Fig. 7]. The sun is coming up. When the sun is coming up it can not yet shine on you directly. I am drawing the apparent process, as we see it. In reality the earth is moving and the sun is standing still, but it does not matter here. So the sun first sends its rays here, and then here. If you are standing there, you do not see the sun at dawn but the illuminated clouds. There are some clouds. And the light is really sitting on those clouds.

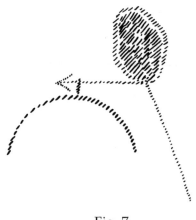

Fig. 7

Well, gentlemen, what is this, really? It it is very instructive. The sun has not yet come up completely and so it is still dark here. All around you it is still dark and there, far away, are the clouds illuminated by the sun. Can you understand that? Standing here you are thus looking through the darkness that surrounds you and seeing the illuminated clouds. You see light through darkness. We are thus able to say: 'At dawn — and it is the same at dusk — we

see light through darkness. And light seen through darkness – you can see this in the rosy dawn or at dusk – is red.'
Light seen through darkness is red. We may say, therefore:
'Seen through darkness, light looks red.' Light seen through
darkness is red.

Now let me tell you something else. Imagine dawn has
passed, it is daytime, and you are looking out into the open
air, the way it is today. What do you see out there? You see
the 'blue sky', as it is called. It is not actually there, but you
do see it. It goes on and on into infinity, but you see it as if it
were a blue shell around the earth. Why is that so?

Well, you only have to consider what it is like out there, in
the far reaches of cosmic space. It is dark out there. The
wide reaches of the cosmos are dark. The sun is shining
only on to the earth, and because there is air around the
earth the sun's rays are caught and create light here
[drawing], especially if they shine through watery air. So if
you stand here in the daytime, looking out into the dark,
you should really be seeing black. But you do not see black
but blue, because the sun is illuminating it all around. The
air and the water in the air are illuminated.

So then you quite clearly see darkness through light. You
look through the light, through the illumination, into the
darkness. We are thus able to say: 'Darkness seen through
light is blue.'

There you have two of the basic laws in the theory of
colour, and you can easily discover them in the world
around you. If you really understand the red dawn and
dusk, you'll say to yourself: 'Light seen through darkness is
red.' If you look out into the black space of heaven in the
daytime, you'll say to yourself: 'Darkness seen through
light – seeing it is light all around you – is blue.'

You see, this perfectly natural way of looking at these
things is something people always had until they became
'clever'. This view – that light through darkness is red,

darkness through light is blue—was held by the ancients over there in Asia, when they were still as clever as I have told you on a recent occasion. The ancient Greeks still held this view. People still held it all through the Middle Ages, until they became clever; until about the fourteenth, fifteenth, sixteenth, seventeenth century. And when they grew clever they began to consider things no longer in their natural way but thought up all kinds of artificial sciences. One man who thought up a particularly artful science of the colours was an Englishman called Newton.[10] Being very clever—you know how I use the term 'clever' now, which is in a completely serious way—being very clever, Newton said something like the following. If we look at the rainbow—for of course, if you are a clever man, you don't look at everyday things like dawn and dusk, when you get clever you look at especially rare things, things one should only understand when one has progressed a bit—well now, Newton therefore said: 'Let us look at the rainbow. We see seven colours in the rainbow—red, orange, yellow, green, blue, indigo, violet.' These are the seven colours one sees in this order in the rainbow [writing them up]. Looking at a rainbow you can easily distinguish these seven colours.

Newton made an artificial rainbow by darkening the room, covering the window with dark paper and making a small hole in the paper. This gave him a very narrow strip of light. Into this strip of light he put something we call a prism. It is a triangular piece of glass, looking like this [Fig. 8]. And he put a screen behind it. So he had the window there, with the hole, this small stream of light, the prism, and behind it the screen. And a rainbow appeared on the screen in red, orange, yellow, green, blue, indigo and violet—all these colours. What did Newton say to himself? Newton said to himself: 'There the white light is coming in; the prism gives me the seven colours of the rainbow. The seven colours of the rainbow are therefore contained in the

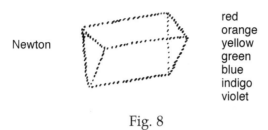

Newton

red
orange
yellow
green
blue
indigo
violet

Fig. 8

white light and I only need to lure them out.' You see, that is the simplest explanation. You explain something by saying it is already present in something from which I then draw it out.

He should really have said to himself: 'Because I am not putting a regular plate of glass [opposite to the screen] but a prism, which has a surface at an acute angle like this, light is made red by darkness on one side, as I look at it. The red colour appears, and on the other side darkness is made blue by light, and the blue appears. And then there are various stages in between.' That is what he should have said to himself.

But at that time the way things went in the world always was that if one wanted to explain something one would look for all of it in the thing out of which one really ought to explain it. You'll agree that is the simplest way of doing it. So to explain how a human being comes into existence, one says: 'Well, he's already there in the egg in his mother, and he merely develops from this.' That is a fine way of explaining things, saying ... [gap in text]. We do not have it so easy, as you've seen. We have to involve the whole of cosmic space, and this then develops the egg from the mother. But modern science seeks to ... [gap in text]. Newton thus said: 'The sun already has all the colours in it, we only have to draw them out.'

But that is not at all the way it is. To produce the red colour at dawn, the sun must first shine on the clouds, and we must see the red through the darkness. And if the sky is to appear blue, this does not come from the sun at all, for the sun does not shine into it. It is black there, dark; and we see the blue through the earth's air which is filled with light. So in that case we see darkness through light and that is blue.

What this means is that we should use proper physics; then people would see how with a prism you see light through darkness on one side, and darkness through light on the other. But they cannot be bothered. They find it best to say: 'Everything is in there in the light, and you just draw it out.' In that case we may also say: 'There was a huge egg once in the world, and the whole world was inside it, and we draw everything from that.' That is what Newton did with the colours. But in reality we can always see the secret of the colours perfectly well if we rightly understand the red dawn and the blue of the sky.

We must now go on and consider the whole thing in relation to the human eye and to human life as a whole. You all know that there is a creature that gets especially excited by red, that is, light acting through darkness. This is the bull. It is known that bulls get terribly excited if they see red. So that is one thing you know. And man also has a bit of bull nature in him. He does not get immediately excited on seeing red, but you will notice right away that someone who is living in a red light all the time does get a bit excited. He becomes a little bit bull-like. I have actually known poets who could not write poetry when their bodies were in their ordinary condition. They would always go and sit in rooms where the lamps had red shades. Afterwards they'd be excited and able to write poetry. Well now, a bull goes wild; and man may even grow poetic in this way, by exposing himself to red. It only depends on whether one does it from the outside or the inside, this livening up to write poetry! So that is the situation on the one hand.

On the other hand you'll also know that when people

who understand such things want to make others who do not understand them especially tame, really humble, they use the colour blue, or the colour black, actually black. In the Roman Catholic Church, for example, when people are meant to grow humble in Advent, the church and above all the vestments are in blue. People grow tame, humble. A person then enters into an inner mood of humility. Especially if he has first been raging like a bull, which might have been the case during the carnival, for example; the proper Lenten fast is made to follow, with not just dark vestments [but actually] black vestments. The person then grows tame, having had his fling. Only the Lenten fast should be twice as long in an area where they in fact have two carnival Sundays. I don't know if that actually happens.[11] But you see from this that it has quite a different effect on people if they perceive light through darkness, i.e. red, or darkness through light, which is blue.

Consider the eye. You have nerves and blood in there. When the eye looks at something red, let us say at the dawn, or anything that is red, what does it experience? You see, when the eye looks at something red, red light passes through these very tiny blood vessels in the eye. And this red light has the peculiar property that it always destroys the blood a little bit. It destroys the nerve as well, for the nerve is only able to live if it is supplied with blood. When the eye comes up against the colour red, when the red comes in, the blood in the eye is always a little bit destroyed, and the nerve too. The bull simply feels, as it sees the colour red: 'Heavens! All the blood in my head is being destroyed! I have to do something to defend myself against this!' So it goes wild, for it does not wish to have its blood destroyed.

Well, this is a very good thing, however, if not for the bull perhaps, but certainly for people and other animals. For if we look at the colour red and our blood is a little bit destroyed, the body will on its part take action and see to it that we get a better supply of oxygen to the eye, so that the blood may be restored again.

Consider the marvellous process that takes place here. When light is seen through darkness, and therefore the colour red, blood is destroyed at first, oxygen is drawn from the body and the eye vitalized with the oxygen. We then know from the way we ourselves get lively in the eye that there is red out there. But if we are to perceive this red, the blood in the eye must first be destroyed a little bit, and the nerve must be destroyed. We have to send life into the eye, that is, send oxygen into it. And from the way our own eye comes alive, from the way it wakes up, we realize that there is red out there.

Now you see, this ability human beings have to perceive light that has turned red, always being able to take in light that has turned red, is really also the basis for their health. For the oxygen taken up from the body will vitalize the whole body, and people will get a healthy colour in their cheeks. They can really come alive.

This is the case not only for someone whose eye is healthy and who is able to see but also for someone whose eye is not healthy and who cannot see. For light is active in bright colours; man then comes alive in his head, and this vitalizing process will in turn affect the whole organism and give it a healthy colour.

It is certainly important, therefore, not to have people grow up in dark rooms where they might become dead and humble, but to let them grow up in bright rooms with red and yellow colour tones. With the help of the light they will then use the oxygen they have inside them to good effect. You can see from this that anything connected with the colour red really has to do with the development of the blood in human beings. The nerve is really destroyed when we perceive the colour red.

Now think of seeing darkness through light, that is, we see

blue. The darkness does not destroy our blood; darkness leaves the blood intact. The nerve also remains intact, because its blood is unaffected. The consequence is that the person feels really well and at ease in himself. He feels really well inside because the blue does not attack his blood and nerves. And people are made humble in a way that is really quite crafty. For if the priests are up there at the altar in their blue vestments, or black vestments, and people are sitting below, looking at them all the time, then the blue vestments do not destroy the small blood vessels and the nerves in the eye, and they will, of course, feel terribly good in there. It is really calculated to make people feel good. Don't think they do not know this! For they do still have the old knowledge. More recent knowledge has only come when people were enlightened, as enlightened as Newton, for example.

We are thus able to say: 'Blue is the colour that makes people feel at ease inside,' so that they say to themselves — all of this is unconscious, but they say to themselves inwardly: 'It is good to live in this blue.' They sense themselves inwardly, whilst if the colour is red they feel as if something is entering into them. For blue we might say that the nerve remains intact, and the body sends its feeling of well-being into the eye and thus into the whole body.

Light through darkness	= red	Blood destroyed. Oxygen drawn in from the body, with the eye vitalized
Darkness through light	= blue	Nerve left intact and body sending feeling of well-being into the eye

You see, that is the difference between blue colours and red colours. Yellow is just a gradation of red, and green a gradation of blue. We are thus able to say that depending on whether nerve or blood is active in a human being, he will be sentient more of red or more of blue.

You see, this can be applied to pigments. So if I want to try and produce a proper red, a red colour for painting, I must produce paint containing substances which stimulate human beings to produce oxygen inside. Bit by bit we then discover that one actually gets red pigment for painting if one tries to find out how much carbon the different materials in the outside world contain. If I use carbon together with other substances in the right way, I discover the secret of getting the colour I use for my painting to be red. So if I use plant materials to produce paints,[12] it is above all important to organize the processes I use — grinding, burning, etc. — in such a way that I then have carbon in the paint in the right way. If I have carbon in it in the right way I get a light, reddish colour. On the other hand if I have materials that contain a lot of oxygen — not carbon, therefore, but oxygen — and I succeed in getting the oxygen into it as oxygen, I get darker colours such as blue.

If I perceive the living principle in the plant, I can truly produce the paints I need from it.

Just imagine I take a sunflower. It is very yellow, and therefore light in colour. Yellow is close to red — light seen through darkness. Now if I treat a sunflower in such a way that I somehow get the proper process that exists in the flower also into my artist's paint, I'll have a good yellow that will stand up well to external light. For the sunflower has stolen the secret of producing yellow from the sun. And if I manage to get the process which exists in the sunflower into my paint, and manage to get it thick enough, I can properly use yellow in my painting.

If I take another plant, a chicory flower, for example, which is blue — it's a blue flower that grows by the wayside; it grows in this area as well — if I have this blue plant and want to produce a pigment for painting from its flower, I find I cannot do it. It will not give me anything. [It will give me something], however, if I process the root in a suitable way; the process which actually makes the flower blue is in there.

If there is yellow in a flower, the yellow is produced in the flower itself. But if there is blue in the flower, the process is located in the root and merely pushes up into the flower from there. So in that case I have to use the root of the indigo plant, which gives me a darker blue, or of chicory, that blue flower. I have to treat it chemically until it yields a blue pigment for me.

In this way I can really study and work out how I may get the pigments from the plants. I cannot do this by following Newton who simply said: 'Ah well, it's all there in the sunlight; I only have to draw it out.' This would at most apply only to a purse. My purse must have all the money in it in the morning that I'll need to spend in the course of the day. This is how the really clever people imagine it to be, like a bag with everything inside it. But that is not the way it is.

You have to know, for instance, how the yellow is in the sunflower or in the dandelion. You have to know how the blue is in the chicory. The processes that produce chicory or indigo blue are located in the root; the processes that make the sunflower or the dandelion flower yellow lie in the flower itself. And so I must develop a live chemistry in which I imitate the flower processes of plants to get light colours and the root processes of plants to obtain dark colours.

You see, what I have been telling you is something that real common sense can discover. This business with the red, orange, yellow, green, blue, indigo and violet of the rainbow, on the other hand, is not something real, fundamentally speaking.

Now the historical event was as follows. In Goethe's lifetime everyone was already believing what Newton had taught: the sun is a big sack, and the seven colours, as they are called, are inside it. You only need to tease them out, and there you have them. Everyone believed that. It was taught then and is still taught today.

Goethe was someone who would not believe everything right away. He always wanted to see the things everyone was taught for himself. People generally say they do not believe in authority, but when it comes to believing in the things taught at the universities they are terribly apt to believe in authority today, believing everything they are taught. Goethe was not prepared to accept things just like that. He therefore borrowed the apparatus used to prove this — a prism or similar apparatus — from Jena University. He clearly thought of doing himself what the professors generally demonstrate, and see for himself how it was.

As it was, Goethe did not immediately find time for this, and kept the apparatus for quite a long while without getting round to using it. And then court counsellor Büttner,[13] who wanted to use the apparatus, ran out of patience and asked for the apparatus to be collected. Goethe then said: 'Now I must have a quick go at this!' He did at least look through the prism as he was packing it up. He said to himself: 'That white wall over there must appear in glorious rainbow colours when I look through it; instead of white there should be red, yellow, green and so on.' So he looked through the prism, looking forward to the colour display, but saw nothing. The wall was as white as ever, simply white. This really surprised him. 'What is behind this?' he asked himself. And you see, this was the beginning of his whole theory of colour. He said: 'I must check the whole thing again. The ancients said: light seen through darkness is red, darkness seen through light is blue. If I vary the red a bit it will be yellow; if I enhance the blue all the way to red, the blue will be green in one direction and violet in the other. These are gradations.' He then developed his theory of colour, and made it better than it had been in medieval times.

And so we now have a physicists' theory of colour with the sack from which the seven colours come, a theory that is taught everywhere, and we have Goethe's theory of colour, where the blue of heaven is properly understood, the red sky at dawn and at night is properly understood, as I have explained it to you just now.

But there is one particular difference between Newton's and Goethe's theories of colour.[14] Other people do not notice it at first, for they are following the physicists. They are taught Newton's theory of colour, which is printed in all the books. One can feel very clever as one pictures the way the red, orange, yellow, green and so on appear in a rainbow. But you see, the situation is that there isn't a prism anywhere! But people don't think about that ... [gap in text]. The Newtonians themselves are aware of this, but they don't admit it even to themselves. For as you look through the rain on the one side, you see the darkness through sunlit rain, you see the blue part of the rainbow on that side. But then one also sees the area in front where light is seen through darkness, and so on the other side one sees the red. So you must explain everything according to one and the same principle—light through darkness is red, darkness through light is blue.

But, as I said, on the one hand people see things the way the physicists explain it to them, and on the other hand they look at paintings produced with pigments. But now they don't ask how it happens that there is red and yellow and so on, they do not put the two things together.

Well, gentlemen, a painter must put the two together. Anyone who wants to paint must put them together. He must not only know: there's a sack, with all the colours in it—for he does not have that sack, nowhere does he have it. But he must find the right way of getting the pigment he needs from the living plant or other living matter, so that he can mix his colours in the right way, he must understand ...

[gap in text]. And so the situation today is that painters really think about these things. There are of course also painters who do not think but just buy their paints. But the painters who think about the way one gets the pigments and how they may use them, they will say: 'Yes, Goethe's theory of colour is something one can work with. It means something to us. As painters we cannot do anything with Newton's theory of colour, the physicists' theory of colour.' The general populace do not put the two things—painting and the physical theory of colour—together, but the painter does! And he'll therefore love Goethe's theory of colour. A painter will say to himself: 'Dear me, those physicists—we don't bother with them. They talk of things in their own field. Let them do what they like. We stick to the old view and to Goethe's theory of colour.' Painters see themselves as artists and do not really think they should intervene in the theories developed by physicists. It would take an effort, and they would meet with opposition, and so on.

That is how things are today with what the books say about colours and the truth of the matter. Goethe simply had to defend the truth, and this drove him to rebel against Newton's physics and the whole of modern physics. And one can have no real understanding of nature without also arriving at Goethe's theory of colour. And so it is of course perfectly natural to have Goethe's theory of colour defended at a Goetheanum. But if you do not limit yourself to some sphere of religion or ethics but dare to intervene in the different subjects in physics, you'll have the whole gang of physicists after you.

So you see, defending the truth is really extraordinarily difficult in our time. But just try and consider the complicated way in which present-day physicists explain the blue colour of the sky! Now of course, if I start from the wrong premise and want to explain such a simple thing as that the blackness of space appears blue if seen through light, I have to produce a terribly complicated explanation. And as to the red sky at dawn or at night! The chapters usually begin by saying: 'Yes, the blue of heaven cannot really be explained today; one might, however, imagine one thing or another.' Yes, the way physicists think of the small hole through which they let light enter into the room, using darkness to examine the light, all this cannot explain even the simplest thing. And so it has come about that people no longer understand anything about colour at all.

If one understands that destruction of the blood and exactly because of this vitalization ... [gap in text] — for if I have blood destroyed by the light in me I call up all the oxygen I have in me, and I come alive, then human health arises. If I have darkness around me, or shades of blue all the time, well, then I want to vitalize myself all the time; I then vitalize myself too much and this very vitalization makes me grow pale, because I stuff myself with too much life. And so we can on the one hand understand the healthy ruddiness of a person from taking up oxygen, when the person really exposes himself to the light; and we can understand paleness as arising from continual carbon dioxide uptake. Carbon dioxide, the opposite of oxygen, wants to get into my head. And that makes me quite pale.

Today you have almost nothing but pale children in Germany for example. But it has to be realized that this comes from an excess of carbon dioxide. And when someone produces too much carbon dioxide — which is a compound of carbon and oxygen — he uses too much of the carbon in him to produce the carbon dioxide [Fig. 9]. So you then have all the carbon such a pale child has in him getting converted into carbon dioxide all the time. This makes him pale. What should I do? I must give him something that will prevent this endless carbon dioxide production inside him, so that the carbon will remain. I can do this by giving him a little calcium carbonate. This will stimulate his functions

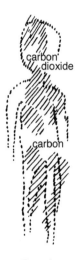

Fig. 9

again—as I have told you before from a completely different point of view—and the individual then keeps the
carbon he needs and does not convert it to carbon dioxide
all the time. And because carbon dioxide consists of carbon
and oxygen, the oxygen goes up to the head and vitalizes
the head processes, the vital processes. If the oxygen is used
up to make carbon dioxide, the vital functions are
suppressed.

So if I take someone who is pale into a region where he
gets a lot of light, he will be stimulated not to give his
carbon up to carbon dioxide, because the light draws the
oxygen up into the head. He'll then develop a healthy
colour again. I can also use calcium carbonate to get this
effect, so that I keep the oxygen and the individual has the
oxygen available to him.

This is how one thing must relate to another. We must be
able to understand health and sickness on the basis of the
theory of colour. You can only do this if you use Goethe's
theory of colour, for this simply fits in with the natural

world in a natural way. You cannot use Newton's theory of colour for this, because it is just an invention and does not relate to the natural world at all. It cannot really explain the simplest things we see — the red sky at dawn and dusk and the blue sky.

There is something else I want to tell you. Think of the pastoral peoples of earlier times who drove their herds and slept in the open. In their sleep they were exposed not to the blue but to a dark sky. And stars beyond number were shining up there in the heavens. Imagine that dark sky therefore, with countless stars shining in it, and down below the sleeping human being. From the dark sky came a calming influence, and the people felt inwardly at ease in their sleep. The whole human being was penetrated by the darkness, growing inwardly calm. Sleep came from the darkness. But there were those stars shining on the people. And wherever a star's ray shone down, the human being became a little bit excited inside. Then a ray of oxygen would go out from the body. And the star rays were all met by rays of oxygen, with the human being having such oxygen rays running through every part of him. He then became an inner oxygen-mirror image of the whole starry firmament [Fig. 10].

The pastoral peoples of old thus took the whole of the starry heavens into their calmed bodies as though in images, images drawn by the rays of oxygen. They would then wake up. And they had the dream of those images. And this gave them their knowledge of the stars. They developed a marvellous science of the stars. They did not dream that the Ram was simply made up of so and so many stars, but they really saw the animal — the ram, the bull and so on — and so felt the whole of the starry heavens to be inside them in images.

This has come down as poetic wisdom to us from those pastoral peoples, a wisdom which sometimes contains extraordinarily many things that can still teach us some-

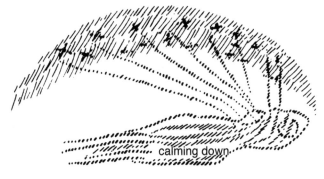

calming down

Fig. 10

thing today. And we can understand this if we know that the human being sends out a ray of oxygen to meet every ray of starlight, and becomes a whole heaven, an inner oxygen heaven.

The inner life of man is a life lived in the astral body, for in sleep he experiences the whole of the heavens. We would be in a sorry state if we had not descended from those pastoral peoples. All human beings are descended from ancient pastoral tribes. We still have an inner starry firmament today, purely by inheritance, to give us insight. We still develop this, though not as well as the ancients did, and in our sleep, lying in our beds, we still have a kind of memory of the way the herds people of old would lie in the fields and receive oxygen into themselves. We aren't pastoral people any more, but we still have something inherited, we still have something, though we cannot give it such beautiful expression because it has grown pale and dim. But the whole of humanity belongs together. And if we want to know the things which people still have in them today we must go back to those earlier times. All human beings everywhere on the earth have come from that pastoral state. And in their bodies they have inherited as much as has still come down to them from those pastoral ancestors.

Dante's view of the world and the dawning of the modern scientific age. Copernicus, Lavoisier

I have been given a question about the colours and asked to say some more about them.

First of all let me consider the question that was asked before that. It concerns the way Dante[15] saw the world. The gentleman has been reading Dante. And when one reads Dante, this medieval writer, one finds that his picture of the world was very different from our own.

Let me ask you to consider the following. People think — I have told you this a number of times — that only the things people know today really make sense. And when they hear of the different ways in which people thought in earlier times they think: 'Ah well, that was in the past.' And so one had to wait until one was able to learn things about the world that made sense.

You see, the things people learn at school today, things about the world that become second nature to them, have really only been like this since Copernicus[16] first thought it up. Following this sixteenth-century idea, people thought the sun was at the centre of our whole planetary system. The heavenly bodies orbiting around the earth are first of all Mercury, then Venus, then the earth [Fig. 11]. The moon orbits around the earth. Then follows Mars, orbiting the sun. Then there are a large number of planets which relative to cosmic space are absolutely tiny and are called planetoids, -oid meaning 'like' planets. Then comes Jupiter, and then Saturn. And then still Uranus and Neptune — I don't need to draw them. That is how people see it today, how it is taught at school — that the sun is standing still at the

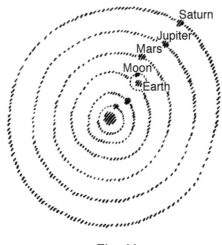

Saturn
Jupiter
Mars
Moon
Earth

Fig. 11

centre. The lines followed by the planets are really a bit elongated. But this does not matter for us today. People think, therefore, that Mercury orbits the sun, then Venus does, and then the earth. As you know, the earth takes a year to move around the sun, 365 days, 6 hours and so on. Saturn goes all the way round once in 30 years, which is much slower than the earth. Jupiter for example takes 12 years, which is also slower than the earth. Mercury moves fairly quickly. The nearer the sun the planets are, therefore, the faster they move.

As you know, that is believed to be the correct view today, and it is taught in the schools. But we only need to go back as far as the fourteenth century, about the year 1300, to find that an extraordinarily great mind like Dante had quite a different idea. So that was a few centuries earlier than Copernicus. And the greatest human being, Dante, the greatest in mind, then had quite a different idea.

We won't decide right away if the one idea or the other is the right one. Let us now look at the way Dante, one of the most important thinkers of his time, saw the matter at that time – it's 1900 now, then it was 1300 – so it was only 600 years ago. Let us not think the one is right and the other wrong, but try and enter into the way Dante saw things. He thought [Fig. 12] that the earth was at the centre of the universe. And this earth is not only such that the moon, for instance, reflects the light it receives from the sun onto the earth, but the earth is not only orbited but is wholly enveloped by the moon sphere. Dante therefore saw the moon as something much bigger than the earth. He saw it as a very subtle, very fine body that is much larger than the earth. It is subtle, therefore, but much bigger. And the object we see is just a little bit of the moon, the solid bit. And this solid bit orbits the earth. Can you visualize this? For Dante the idea was that the earth was inside the moon, and the bit we see of the moon is only a tiny, solid part of it. That moves in orbit. But in reality we are all of us inside the powers of the moon. I have drawn this in red.

And the way Dante saw things was like this: if the earth were not within those powers of the moon, human beings might one day come to the earth by some kind of miracle, but they would not be able to procreate. The reproductive powers are in the sphere I have drawn in red. They also stream through the human being, and make human beings capable of reproducing themselves. Dante therefore imagined the earth to be a small, solid body; the moon he thought was a subtle body – much more subtle than air – a large subtle body, with the earth inside it like a kernel. You can imagine the earth like a plum stone in the soft fruit pulp of the plum. And out there is the solid bit; this moves in orbit. But this [Fig. 12, moon sphere] is also always present, and it is because of this that human beings are able to reproduce themselves, and animals, too, are able to reproduce themselves.

He also considered the following. The earth is not only

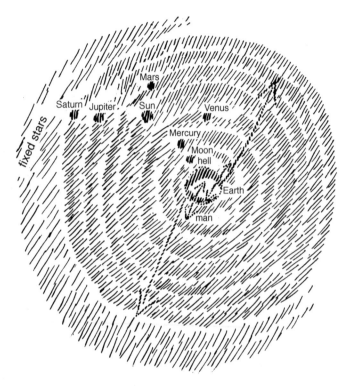

Fig. 12

inside the moon powers but it is also inside other powers —
I'll make them yellow here — and they penetrate all the rest
of it. So you have the moon powers in there, and earth and
moon are both inside this yellow sphere. And again we
have a solid part. This solid part is the planet Mercury
which orbits out there. And if human beings did not have
the powers of Mercury in them all the time they would not
be able to digest. Dante therefore thought the powers of the
moon made reproduction possible, the powers of Mercury — and we are also always inside them, only they are
more subtle than the moon powers — make it possible for us
to digest our food, and for animals to digest their food.

Otherwise we would just have a chemical laboratory in our bodies, he thought. It is due to the powers of Mercury that things go differently in our bodies than they do in a chemical laboratory where substances are merely mixed together and then separated again. This is due to the powers of Mercury. Mercury is thus larger than the earth and larger than the moon.

And now everything is inside another sphere, as Dante called it, which is even bigger. So we are also within the powers that come from this planet, from Venus. We are thus inside all those powers, and they enter into us. Because we have Venus forces in us we are able not only to digest but also to take anything we have digested into the blood. Venus powers live in our blood. Everything that has to do with the blood in us comes from the powers of Venus. That is how Dante saw it. And these Venus powers create any feelings of love human beings have in their blood—hence the name Venus.

The next sphere is one we are also inside, and here the sun moves around us as a solid part of it. We are thus completely within the sun. For Dante in the year 1300, the sun was not just the body that rises and goes down; his sun was present everywhere. Standing here I am inside the sun. For the body that rises and sets, and moves along over there is only part of the sun. That is how he saw it. And the powers of the sun are above all active in the human heart.

So there you have it. Moon, human and also animal reproduction; Mercury, human digestion; Venus, development of human blood; sun, human heart.

And Dante then thought that all of this was inside the vast Mars sphere. There is Mars. And just as the sun is connected with the human heart, so Mars—and we are also inside this—is connected with everything to do with speech and everything we have by way of breathing organs. That is in Mars. Mars, then—breathing organs. And there is more of it. The next sphere is the Jupiter sphere. We are also inside the Jupiter powers. Jupiter is, of course, very important; it has to do with everything that is our brain, really our sense organs, our brain with the sense organs. Jupiter is thus connected with the sense organs. And then comes the outermost planet, which is Saturn. Everything is again inside this. And Saturn has to do with our organ of thinking.

Moon	human reproduction
Mercury	human digestion
Venus	human blood development
Sun	human heart
Mars	breathing organs
Jupiter	sense organs
Saturn	thinking organs

So you see that this man Dante, who was only 600 years before us, saw the whole universe in a different way. He believed Saturn, for instance, to be the biggest of the planets in which we are. And those Saturn powers create our thinking organs, they make it possible for us to think.

Now beyond all this, but again in such a way that we are inside it, is the firmament of fixed stars. Those then are the fixed stars, and above all the zodiac [Fig. 12]. And even greater is that which sets it all in motion, the prime mover. This is not only up there, however, but is also the prime mover everywhere here. And beyond it lies eternal rest, a calm that also exists everywhere else. That is how Dante saw it.

Well now, someone may come today and say: 'That is the way it is; people saw everything imperfectly then. But today we have finally reached the point where we know how things are.' Sure, that is what one might say. But Dante was not exactly stupid, and he also saw the things people see today. So he was not exactly stupid. And the others, from whom he took his ideas, people who all held that belief at the time, were not exactly silly people either. It is just that they had different ideas about it. And the question is, how has it happened in the history of the world that people thought differently about the whole nature of the universe in earlier days, and then suddenly turned everything upside down in the sixteenth century and developed a completely different idea of the world?

This is, of course, a very important question, gentlemen. And you will not get anywhere by saying, oh well, those earlier ideas were childish. For those people did see things very differently from the way people see them today. This is something we must understand. They saw something very different. Modern people are able to think so terribly well. And those earlier people were not able to think as well as people do today. Thinking is really something that has only developed gradually. The people of those earlier times had a terrible fear of Saturn, which is connected with the organ of thinking. Saturn, they thought, ruins the human being. It is not good to think too much. Saturn was always considered to be a dark planet. And they thought the powers that came from Saturn would make people quite melancholic if they became too powerful in them. They would then think all the time and grow melancholic. So they were not too keen on the Saturn powers, and tended to visualize things more in images. They did not calculate so much. Today we calculate everything. Copernicus' image of the world has all been calculated. Those earlier people did not make calculations. But they knew something else, something modern people do not know. They knew that powers were active everywhere in the world, wherever you looked. But these powers, which are also in the human being, are not in the world we see with our eyes; they are in the invisible realm.

And so Dante said to himself: 'There is a visible world,

and an invisible world. The visible world — well, it is the one we see. Looking out there at night we see the stars, the moon, Venus, and so on. That is the visible world. But there is also the invisible world.' And the invisible world consists in those spheres, as they called them in the old days. And they distinguished the world one sees with one's eyes, and called it the physical world. That was the physical world. And they distinguished the world one does not see with one's eyes. That is the world Dante was thinking of, and it was called the etheric world. That was the etheric world, the world which consists of such subtle matter that one is always looking right through it.

Well now, gentlemen, I do not know if you have come across this, but I have known people who insisted that there is no such thing as air, for one cannot see it. They would say: 'Well, if I go from A to B, there is nothing there; I am not walking through anything there.' You know that there is air there, and I walk through it. But, as I said, I have known people who did not have the education which modern people have, and they did not believe that there is any air; they would say: 'There's nothing there.' Dante knew that there is also not just air, but moon, Venus, and so on. It is just the same. You say: 'I am moving through air.' Dante would say: 'I am walking through the moon, I am walking through Venus, I am walking through Mars.' That is the whole difference. And all the things one does not see in the ordinary way, and which one is also unable to detect with the usual physical and chemical apparatus — all this was called the etheric world. Dante was therefore speaking of a very different world, an etheric world. And why was it that Dante saw the world differently 600 years ago? It was because he wrote of something else, he wrote of the invis- ible realm, of the etheric world. And all that Copernicus said was: 'Let us forget the etheric world and describe the physical world. For that is progress.' So you should not think that Dante was a clown, for he was simply writing about the etheric and not the physical world. The physical world was not particularly important to him. He wrote about the etheric world.

Now you see, the whole only changed to any major extent at the end of the eighteenth century. Up to the end of the eighteenth century people always still knew something about this etheric world. In the nineteenth century they no longer knew of it. We are discovering it again through anthroposophy. In the nineteenth century people knew nothing of this etheric world.

Concerning your other question—
If we go back to the eighteenth century, we find people did the following, for example. They would say: 'Here we have a candle, with its wick. And the candle is burning.' Now you know that when a candle burns it is bluish at the centre, and yellowish around the edges [Fig. 13]. You can explain

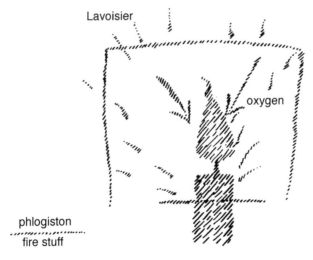

Fig. 13

this very nicely because of the things we have said about the colours. You see, at the centre it is dark, and here it is light [around the outer edge]. And the result is that you see darkness through light. And you know, for I told you this the other day, when we see darkness through light it looks blue. The inside of a candle flame therefore looks blue, because we see darkness through light. I just wanted to draw your attention to this, so that you may see that the ideas and views about colour I have told you the last time apply in every case.

Now you know that when a candle burns it gets less and less. Up above is the flame, and the candle material which melts here [on the candle] goes into the flame. In the end the candle has gone. The material of the candle has spread out into the air.

Now imagine someone who lived, let us say, in 1750, which is not quite 200 years ago. He would say: 'Right, if the candle burns there and it all goes into the air, something of the candle goes into open space. Nothing is left of it in the end. And so the whole candle must go out into open space.' He would also say: 'It consists of some subtle material, fire stuff. This fine fire stuff unites with the flame and goes off in all directions. So in 1750 someone would still say: 'Inside the wax is some stuff that has merely been squashed together, made denser. When the flame makes it into fine matter it goes out into open space.' The stuff was called 'phlogiston' in those days. Something therefore comes away from the candle. The fire stuff, the phlogiston, comes away from the candle.

Then someone else came at the end of the eighteenth century and said: 'No, I do not really believe that there is a phlogiston that goes off into the world. I don't believe it!' What did he do? He did the following. He also burned the whole thing, but he did it in such a way that he captured everything that evolved. He burned it in an enclosed space, so that he was able to capture anything that might evolve. And then he weighed it. And he found that the whole did not grow less in weight. So he had first weighed the whole candle, and then the little bit that was left when the candle had burned down to there [drawing]; and he captured anything that developed in the burning process, weighed it and found that it was a little bit heavier than before. When something burns, he said, whatever evolves does not grow lighter but heavier.

And the person who did this was Lavoisier.[17] Why was it that he took such a different view? It was because he was using scales, because he weighed everything. And he then said: 'If it is heavier, it cannot be that something went away, but something must have been added. And that is oxygen.' Before that, people had thought phlogiston was flying away, and afterwards people thought that if something burns, oxygen comes in, and in combustion one does not have phlogiston dispersing, but oxygen actually being drawn in. This has come about because Lavoisier was the first to weigh these things. Before that, people did not weigh them.

You see, gentlemen, it is as plain as can be what really happened there. By the end of the eighteenth century people no longer believed in anything that could not be weighed. Phlogiston was of course something they could not weigh. Phlogiston did go off. Oxygen did come in. But the oxygen could be weighed when it combined with other matter. Phlogiston could not be captured. Why? Well all the things Copernicus observed when he studied Mars and Jupiter are things that are heavy when you weigh them. The body Copernicus called Mars would weigh something if you put it on some really big scales. So would the body he called Jupiter. He only looked at the bodies that had weight.

Dante did not just look at bodies that had weight but rather at things that had the opposite of weight, things that forever want to go out into cosmic space. And phlogiston simply belongs to the things Dante observed, whilst oxygen belongs to the things Copernicus observed. Phlogiston is the invisible principle that disperses, the ether. Oxygen is a substance you can weigh.

So you see how materialism came into existence. This is something that may become extraordinarily important for you. Materialism arose because people began to believe only in the things that could be weighed. The things Dante still saw could not be weighed. If you walk about on this earth, we can weigh you as well. You have weight, and if you consider the human being to be only the part that has weight, all you have is the earthly human being. But remember, this earthly human being will be a corpse one day. Everything that has weight, that can be treated with scales, will be a corpse. Then the corpse lies there. You will still be able to live in the part that does not have weight, the part that exists around this earth and which materialists say does not exist. Dante still spoke of it and we'll have to speak of it again, of the fact that it exists. We are thus able to say: when a human being lays aside his outer, heavy body, which can be weighed, he remains at first in the ether body.

And now I am going to tell you what is actually there in the ether body. You see, if there is a chair here I can see that chair. I have a picture inside me of this chair. But I don't see it any more when I turn round. But the picture of it is still inside me, still a real picture. It is the memory picture.

Now think of memory pictures. Think of some event you saw and heard quite a long time ago. Say you were in some place, saw cheerful people dancing in the market square, and so on. I could equally well mention some other thing. You have retained that picture. The event you have as a picture no longer exists, gentlemen, and above all it is not among the things one can weigh. It can only be visualized in you. You may go about today and, if you have a lively imagination, have a clear idea of how it all went, even the colours worn by those who were leaping about. You have the whole picture before your mind's eye. But you would never think for a moment that one can weigh the things you saw once long ago. This thing here you can put on the scales. Individual people have weight. But the memory picture you have in you cannot be put on any scales. That is not possible. It has remained with you, though physically the matter no longer exists. How does it come to be inside you, this memory picture? It is in you etherically. No longer physically, but etherically.

Now imagine you have gone for a swim, and because of some mishap you are close to drowning; but you are saved. People who have almost died from drowning and have been saved have generally told others of a most interesting memory picture they had. It is also possible to have this memory picture if one is not about to drown but trains oneself in the science of the spirit, in anthroposophy. The people who were close to drowning had a review of their whole life, right back to their childhood. Everything rises before the mind's eye. Suddenly there is this memory picture. Why? Well, gentlemen, because the physical body, which is now in the water, goes through a very special process. And here you have to recall something I have told you on another occasion. I told you that if you have water and a body in it, the body grows lighter in the water [Fig. 14]. It loses as much weight as a body of water of the same size.

A nice story is told of how this was discovered. The discovery that a body always grows lighter in water was made in ancient Greece. Archimedes[18] gave a lot of thought to these things. And one day he was having a bath. People were absolutely astonished — yes, when you took a bath in Greece, other people were able to look on — people were absolutely astonished when Archimedes suddenly leapt

Fig. 14

from his bath and shouted: 'Eureka! Eureka!' That means: 'I've got it!' People thought: what has he found in his bath? He had immersed himself in the bath, leaving just the head out. He raised a leg above the water and found that when he put his leg out of the water it grew heavier; when he put it down into the water again, it got lighter. This is what he was the first to discover in his bath. It is known as Archimedes' principle.

Every body is therefore lighter in the water. And when someone is drowning his physical body grows light, very light. The memories he has in his ether body continue, and they will all come up at this point. And you see they come up because he is no longer so heavy. When human beings die they are completely outside their physical bodies, and this means they are very light. They then live wholly in the ether sphere. After their death they thus remember everything they lived through on earth, all the way back to their childhood. The first experience we have after death is this complete memory.

We can test this memory. We can do so by taking up the training I have described in my book *Knowledge of the Higher Worlds*.[19] We can then always have this complete memory. We know that the soul grows independent of the body. It then first of all has this memory, for it does not, to begin with, live in the matter we are able to lay aside but rather in something that wants to go out into the whole wide world. That is the first state after death. You remember. The second

Now you may well say that there are animals that use their forelimbs in a way similar to human beings, apes for example, and also other creatures. Well, you must always remember that an ape is really not very skilful in its front limbs relative to its whole organization. It may not always touch the ground with its forelimbs, but it does have need to hold on to something with them. And when it does not hold on, when it is not climbing, it is definitely clumsy. It cannot use its forelimbs in the right way. Most animals walk on all fours, however, and human beings also walk on all fours to start with. They must first find their balance in learning to walk. This is something human beings have to learn in life—first of all, they must learn to walk.

Secondly, as you all know, human beings learn something animals do not get to do, or at least not in the same way. Only someone whose ideas are divorced from reality would say that animals get to do it the same way. It is human speech. I won't say that animals are not able to communicate. I have told you enough things to show that animals are able to communicate. But they do not do so by speaking. They will sniff one another or something like that, but they do not communicate by speech. The second thing a human being has to learn, therefore, is to talk.

The third thing a human being has to learn, again something animals do not develop in the same degree, is thinking. These are the three things a human being must learn—to walk, to talk and to think.

You may say: 'Ah, but surely we can't easily tell the thinking which a human being does from the thinking of an animal. We simply don't know if animals aren't able to think as well.' But someone who says we are unable, well from just looking at animals, to know if they do not think is more or less like someone who says: 'If my grandmother had four wheels and a steering rod up front, she'd be a bus!' One can of course say anything if one does not consider the facts. One can of course say, if one does not consider the facts: 'Why should not a stone speak as well, or think?' But if you consider the facts the situation is that animals do everything in such a way that the sense that lives in them is not personal but cosmic. They do not do it personally; because of this the things they do may be much more sensible, but they are not personal. They think a great deal, as we have heard, but their thinking is not personal.

You see, these three things are something human beings must first learn—to walk, to talk and to think.

A normally developing child will first learn to walk, then to talk, and only then to think. It is quite wrong to think that people think before they talk; they first learn to talk by imitating others. They imitate the words they hear, and it is only in those words that they learn to think. Man learns to think by using speech. This is why the whole of humanity only learned to think at such a late date. The primitive peoples did talk, but people only learned to think later on. They learned to think by using speech.

Consider what the whole of human life would be like if man did not learn to walk, talk and think in his childhood. But you'll also realize that man needs a body to do these three things—walking, talking and thinking. This is perfectly obvious in the case of walking. The whole way the body is made shows you that man needs his body to be able to walk. You cannot even imagine someone walking without a body. Human beings therefore need a body to be able to walk. As to talking—well, I have told you how speech evolves—human beings need a larynx for this, a tongue and all kinds of things. So they need their bodies to be able to talk. And they also need their bodies to be able to think. They need their brains and their nervous systems for this. You can easily investigate this. If someone is not able to think well and you examine the brain, you will find that it has turned to mush. The human being therefore needs his body specifically for the things he learns on earth.

But we need to understand what really happens when we walk, for example, and when we move altogether. When we move in any way, part of us is always perishing. If I stand here and just walk over there, and if I were to examine my body after taking those steps, I would find more ash in my body than it contained before. This is because substances have been burned in it. I cannot move at all, cannot relate to balance, to gravity, unless I burn something or other inside myself. I must therefore bring about combustion inside myself when I use the ability I gain with walking and with movement in the proper sense altogether. Now if I were to be active all the time and would therefore all the time burn things inside me, well, then I'd soon perish. I must all the time also restore the things I have burned.

But you see, the outside world does not do this for me. The outside world does not restore the things I have burned inside me. For you only have to look at a human corpse to see this. This has been completely given over to the outside world, which destroys it by combustion. The outside world burns the body up. You'll say: 'Well, not all people are cremated, some are also buried.' But the decomposition that happens in the grave is merely a slow burning process. It is exactly the same process. If one quickly cremates a body, it burns up in a short time. Someone put in a grave will burn slowly. It always is a real combustion process, as I explained when I spoke of a candle the last time, only on one occasion the body is burned quickly, totally, and on the other occasion the body burns slowly in the grave.

So when we give ourselves to the earth as corpses, we burn. And we also burn when we walk, when we move. Now we cannot bring the corpse back to life, for we are unable to use it for the other process which compensates for the combustion. We would be able to bring a corpse back to life at any time if we were able to reverse the combustion process. Now you see, this is something we are able to do for as long as we live. Then we are really able to reverse the combustion process. Why? If we only had the body that is laid in the grave, we would not be able to reverse the combustion effect. Apart from the body that is laid in the grave we also have an ether body. This is a subtle body. So to do a proper drawing of the human being we have first of all his physical body and then his ether body [Fig. 15]. Having an ether body we are quite rightly able to make good the combustion caused by our movements. And so we do not just have a physical body, we also have an ether body. When we are sleeping, the ether body is all the time

Fig. 15

mending the damage caused by combustion processes in the course of the day. This means that we also have our ether body when we are asleep. It is therefore the physical body and the ether body of the human being which lie in the bed.

Now, how does the ether body differ from the physical body? You can feel this. It is gravity which causes the combustion in you when you give yourself up to the outside world. And the ether body does not have gravity. If we now really think of the thoughts that we are able to recall, we have to say that they do not belong to the physical body, they belong to the ether body. And the situation is that in his ability to remember man is not subject to gravity. You can work and think at the same time, though it is difficult — but that is due to something else. We may discuss it later. But we can work and think at the same time. Everyone knows this, because work will in the first place only wear down the physical body. The ether body is not worn down by physical work. This is the important point. The ether body works in such a way in the human being that in this ether body the human being has something which in the first place enables him to have recall, to have memory.

Now let us go on to the second thing a human being is able to learn — speech. When we learn to talk it is not the same as it is with walking. When we do physical work we also move about in the outside world. We relate to the something or other in the outside world which offers perceptible resistance. Speech is something we produce and we do not really find that talking gets difficult if the air is heavy or stale. Other things make us notice what the air does to us when it is stale and upsets us. We do not notice it in the process of talking. And yet, we would not be able to talk if it were not for the air, for we move the air when we speak.

Combustion processes in us are not only related to outer work, for when you eat something this must first of all go through your mouth into your stomach. There it has to be processed. Then it must become part of the whole body. This is inner work; it, too, burns up the physical body. If the ether body were to be inactive for just a moment — well, that would be the end of it for the person. He would then kill himself all the time with those combustion processes inside him. Everything a person does in this world is really designed to kill.

It is not like this when we talk. If someone were to stop his heart function for a moment, that is, if the combustion caused by the activity of the heart were not immediately made good again by the ether body, the heart would stop beating. But we cannot say the same about speech. Quite the contrary. Someone who talks all the time would soon arouse our loathing. And he would not exactly be helping himself either. When it comes to speech, it is not the case that people should talk all the time. They may talk, if they wish, but they may also let up. But they cannot let up when it comes to the ether body balancing out the activity of the heart. This is something they must do from the beginning to the end of their life on earth.

There is a big difference, therefore, between the things we do inwardly when we speak and those we do just to live. We talk when we wish to do so. But we also destroy something inside us when we talk. We really destroy something. You see, when we breathe we are all the time taking in oxygen, combining the oxygen with the blood, and releasing carbon dioxide. We do not have the same kind of use for nitrogen. But when we talk we always take in too much nitrogen. The strange thing about talking is that we take in too much nitrogen. We poison ourselves in a way. Taking in too much nitrogen means getting more similar to cyanide. For cyanide is a compound of carbon and nitrogen, just as carbon dioxide is a compound of carbon and oxygen. A person is constantly cyanizing himself when he talks.

And this, too, must be balanced out. When someone sets his organs of speech in motion he kills himself, in a way, just as he kills himself with the combustion that develops through movement. This needs to be balanced out. And this is done by the astral body. Please don't worry about the term 'astral'. I might also use another term. It is immaterial. So this is what the astral body does. This astral body is also present in the human being, and it lives in our breathing and speech.

And you can now see the big difference between the astral body and the ether body. If we did not continue to make up for the combustion that has happened during the day even when we are asleep at night, we would not sleep but die. We must therefore always leave the ether body with the physical body during life on earth. We cannot talk when we are asleep at night; we'd first have to wake up. Talking has to do with the astral body. And so we simply withdraw the astral body from the physical and ether bodies during the night. Because of this we also breathe a little bit differently during the night. We exhale less carbon dioxide during the night than we do in the day. In short, we have a third body in us, an astral body [Fig. 15]. And the astral body lives in our speech.

Looking at an animal we note it can walk, too; it can move around, only it does not have to learn this but has it instinctively. But when you look at the animals you find that they cannot talk. They do also have organs of speech. It should really surprise us that a dog does not talk, that it merely barks. It cannot use its astral body to talk. It does not learn to talk. As human beings we must therefore learn to move, to walk, and we must learn to talk. The animal learns nothing for its ether body, learns nothing for its astral body. But we human beings learn things.

Now you see, the fact that we are able to learn something is due to the fact that we have thoughts. All learning consists in having thoughts. To talk, the human being merely needs to imitate. To think, he must be active himself. Man learns through thoughts, therefore. He also learns to walk and he learns to talk through thoughts; only he does not yet know it. He does not yet have the thoughts when he walks and talks. And we are able to learn, which is something animals cannot do, due to the fact that apart from the physical, the ether and the astral body we also have an I, which is present in every part of us. So we also have an I [Fig. 15]. Those, then, are the four aspects of the human being—physical body, etheric body, astral body and I.

What I have just told you is based on looking at the whole human being in the right way, a truly scientific way. Ordinary science is not truly scientific. It does not care about the real facts. It is quite clear that everyone who really learns anything at all would have to say: the human being has a physical body, an ether body, an astral body and an I. But he does not say so, for people simply do not care to consider the facts.

Let us now consider what really happens when we die. You see, this is something one cannot really consider unless one takes the learning process a bit further than is usually done today. The situation is that today's civilized people, as they call themselves, are terribly lazy. What do these civilized people do? It is altogether of little interest to them that a human being learns to walk, for it just happens when a child imitates the grown-ups. No particular attention is paid to this.

Nor does it surprise people that human beings learn to talk. There was a time on this earth when human beings could not talk at all. They had a kind of sign language. Then human beings learned to talk. But this is something humanity has long since forgotten. The study of history today simply consists in considering early human beings who were already able to talk. And people take no interest in the fact that speech is something else we have to learn by doing. This is why nation goes against nation. If they were ever to discover that they have learned to talk, and that speech is something human beings have learned, they would not be so arrogant about language and speech, nor want to be separate nations. People have completely forgotten that speech is something that has to be learnt out of our inner being.

Now when one wants to come into anthroposophy, then, I'd say, one has to learn one's language all over again. For you'll find that when someone gives a talk nowadays — wow, it's as if it comes from a machine. Observe it — you'll find it is as if it were coming from a machine. It is different from the way it is when someone gives a talk about something out of the science of the spirit, out of anthroposophy. There one must all the time try and find the words, take them up again in a new way inwardly. And then, having shaped the words, one really begins to worry that they did not really present things correctly. In anthroposophy, the relationship to those who listen to one is very different than it is with academics today. Modern academics no longer take care with their speech. In anthroposophy, one must always take care of speech and language.

You see, this is something that shows itself especially when I write my books nowadays; I then find myself in a constant state of inner unrest, I would say, concerned to shape the language in such a way that people may also understand what is being written. Something new has to be created here, using language. Modern academics simply say, 'My style is poor; I don't write very well,' for they are used to putting one word after the other, the way we use the mechanics of walking. And so they are not accustomed to someone shaping his sentences a bit differently from the way they do it. And you can see that people today do not care much about language.

And now the third thing, thinking. Well, modern people are particularly proud of their thinking. But I would say that people do not think at all today. People usually do not think at all today. Let me give you an example to show that people do not think at all today. We can see this if we take religion, for example. Religions exist. And yet, they did not always exist. People have only come to religion in the course of evolution. And if you really study history, you'll see how people struggled to develop their religious convictions. This is why in earlier times such a thing as struggling to gain religious convictions did exist. What do people do today? They accept the old religious elements as their inheritance. But they do not want to take in new ideas about things beyond the world of the senses or the like. If human beings had always been like that they'd still be beasts today—for that is the truth—because they'd never have taken thought about anything beyond the world of the senses. Today people are unable to take in ideas about anything supersensible. They will only take in what has been preserved in the churches, thoughts people have been thinking in earlier times. Scientists will of course tell you that they are quite independent of the church and develop their own ideas. That is not true. For if you know the church you'll see that the ideas academics have today are merely the ideas that were developed in the church in earlier times.

Some time ago there was a great scholar in Berlin. His name was Du Bois-Reymond.[20] He really was a great scholar. Above all he was a very elegant speaker, for it all went quite mechanically, it was inherited—just as your great-aunt likes it if the vicar says things she's already familiar with in his sermon; she'd probably not like it so much if he were to say anything new, and she'd fall asleep over it. Du Bois-Reymond, then, a great scholar, made a major speech at a naturalists' gathering in Leipzig in the 1870s. This speech has become very famous. He said, more or less, that as human beings we can understand the things we perceive through the senses. We do not understand things that go beyond the senses. This we do not know. The speech has become famous as the '*Ignorabimus* speech' — *ignorabimus* means: we'll never know anything. That was his conclusion: we'll never know.

Now why did Du Bois-Reymond make that speech? If one of you had gone there and said to him: 'You are a pupil' — or, if you like, one of you might have said: 'Your excellency, you are a pupil — of Thomas Aquinas, one of the Church Fathers!' Du Bois-Reymond would have gone as red as a beetroot and been really upset at being told he was a pupil of Thomas Aquinas, a teacher of the Roman Catholic Church. This would not have been to his liking. He did say in another speech: 'German scholars are a scientific body-guard of the Hohenzollerns.'[21] He was speaking of the scholars of whom he is one. But even if he cheerfully acknowledged the House of Hohenzollern, he would not have acknowledged Thomas Aquinas.

But, you see, what did Thomas Aquinas teach? He also taught that man is able to perceive the world of the senses by himself; that he needed the revelation given by the Church to gain insight into the supersensible world, being unable to find this for himself. Just take out the words 'revelation given by the Church' from this and you have exactly what Du Bois-Reymond was teaching. He merely took out one bit because it gave him some discomfort. He is indeed a pupil of Thomas Aquinas. For it is not at all true that modern science has its own ideas. It also takes up the ideas of the Church. It is just that people do not realize this. It is only through anthroposophy that people are again developing their own ideas. Generally people do not realize that they have no ideas of their own.

And so today no one pays attention to the fact that people learn to walk, to move; that people learn to talk;

and that they learn to think. For that is how it is. If you pay attention to the way speech is shaped out of the inner human being, if you pay attention to the way in which combustion has to be made up for from inside us, and if you pay attention to the way in which thinking in particular takes shape in the inner human being, you arrive at the eternal, immortal element in the human being. But if we pay no attention to these things at all, it is easy to see why we cannot arrive at the eternal, the immortal part. You see, it is due to thoughtlessness and lack of attention when it comes to human speech and walking that people are quite unaware that they have something in them that makes them more than a corpse which is put in a grave when they die. They have to fight this corpse all the time; otherwise they'll die any minute. And they must fight it through their ether body, their astral body and their I. Human beings thus must fight death all the time inside themselves. Death is ever-present. We might die at any moment. But we do not die for as long as we are able to connect our ether body, astral body and our I in the right way, both in our sleep and when awake.

What, then, remains for us in death? In the first place the ether body remains. But this ether body is powerfully attracted to the world. It does not have weight, it does not have gravity. But it wants to expand the moment it is free, the moment we cease to live. What does this mean? It means we extract the ether body. But the moment we extract the ether body we must die, for it is, after all, the body that enables us to live. To die thus means in the first place to extract the ether body from the physical body. Then the physical body really begins to burn up, for the ether body is no longer inside it. At the same time the ether body seeks to expand into the whole world. Because of this, human beings still have memory after death, for, as I have told you, this is bound to the ether body. But the ether body will rapidly expand into the whole world. This means that this memory will be gone after a few days. For a few days, therefore, human beings have a memory of their past life on earth, which is just the way it is with someone who is drowning. I explained this to you the other day. You see, this is what someone who is an anthroposophist will say; he does not invent it, so what is it that he does? Well, he learns something in addition to the things we usually learn. People walk about in everyday human life today. They walk, which means they see how they are constantly burning up. But they never look to see how this is made good again. If they were to observe how the combustion is made good again—that is, what happens if I just move my foot and must then use the ether body to pour compensation for the combustion into it—they would begin to perceive the ether body. But people forget this today. They do not direct their attention to the ether body. But that is the learning process in anthroposophy. You learn to note how a process that goes against death is continually developed in the human being. And then one makes experiments just as people do experiments in physics and chemistry laboratories. Let me describe such an experiment for you. I have described the whole method in my book *Knowledge of the Higher Worlds.*[22] But let me show you once more how one does these things.

Imagine therefore that I have done something or other during the day, some kind of work, which may have been more physical or more mental. At night, before going to sleep, one puts this very clearly before the mind's eye: there, that's you, this fellow. But you see him outside yourself. And then you visualize how you moved your legs, moved your hands, what you were thinking—all this you bring to mind. And when you thus recall it, quite a different idea will gradually come of its own accord; it is an idea of how it all needs to be made good again. You get an idea of your ether body, a little bit of your ether body. This is certainly something you can call forth.

People today will say: 'Ah well, it is enough if one learns to look at outside life.' No care is taken to see that children also get to know something else at school. That is the easiest way. For people who get to know more grow rebellious. If we developed just this one faculty when children are still in their tenderest youth, all people would be able to perceive the ether body.

You see, you may have done tremendous exercises to perceive the things you yourself do as you move about, as you work — this may also be mental work. You may get very clear ideas, but the whole is undone again, for after three days those ideas will have gone. When you learn something about the physical world, swot it up, it will stay with you if you swotted it up properly. The ideas you develop of the supersensible world, doing it in the ether body, will have gone after three days; they will have gone unless you have first made them into physical notions. Why? Because it is just as if one is producing artificially, in an experiment, what will happen after death. The etheric images slip away after death. And they'll also slip away if one produces them artificially. You can get to know this through the science of the spirit, doing the right kind of experiments on yourself, just as with physical science you get to know the compounds of oxygen, let us say, in the laboratory. But this means that we must not stop at ordinary science. And my book *Knowledge of the Higher Worlds* therefore takes the things people learn further, but takes them further the way it does this fact — that a human being only has those experiences in the ether body for two or three days. This fact can be established again, and it then becomes science.

Well, you see, that is how we can experience the ether body. But it is also possible to experience the astral body. When someone looks at some water, he does not normally know right away that it contains hydrogen and oxygen. He must use a galvanic apparatus to separate the two substances. He then has hydrogen and oxygen in two containers side by side. And if we want to perceive the astral body we must first be able to separate it from the physical body. We thus have to work in a truly scientific way for this. For example one has to observe: 'You took some water, drank some water, at a particular time of the day. Then you did not drink any for a long time. You grew thirsty.' When one gets thirsty one wants to drink again. This is exactly as you must want speech to come before speech actually appears. It is exactly the same. With speech, we have to want to speak; when we are thirsty, we want to drink. Thirst means no more and no less but that one wants to drink. This is the will to drink. We may thus say that one discovers with self-observation that one gets desires, that real desires arise. Please note. First we have memory. Memories will sometimes come if we will this, but most of the time they come of their own accord. They rise up, those memories. They are connected with the ether body. Our desires — thirst, hunger or desires in mind and soul — rise up in such a way in the human being that they are like willing something. The will of the human being comes to expression in them. The desire will continue until it is satisfied, until the will has been given its due.

But note carefully what it is one really wills when one is thirsty, for instance. What is it we will in that case? When we are thirsty, we want water to circulate in there the way water does circulate in the body. We are thirsty because it is not circulating. So what is it that we really want then? We want our body to be functioning in the proper way. When we are hungry we also want the body to be functioning in a particular way. So we really always want something that has to do with ourselves. And you see, this something which we want to be like that in ourselves is something the body cannot bring about. You know, if the body had to work all the time to meet desire, it would have to consume itself in the process. The body cannot develop desire.

So where do desires come from? They come from the soul. They do not come from the ether body. Something like memory comes from the ether body. Desires come from the astral body. And desire is not always there, whilst life, coming from the ether body, is always there. Desire alternates with satisfaction, because it belongs to the astral body. That is how we discover the connection between desire and the astral body.

What, then, does desire seek to achieve? It wants to have the astral body in a particular condition. Now by learning more in the way I have told you when talking of learning things connected with the ether body, we can also learn more with regard to our desires. Strangely enough, as we continue the learning process, we go further and further back in life and come to the point where we were in childhood. There we had nothing but desires. At the time which we no longer remember, we had nothing but desires. The infant kicks and struggles, has nothing but desires. A child is sheer desire when it comes into the world. And we go back to that desire. There we get to know the astral body.

You do not get to know your astral body unless you use the methods I have described in *Knowledge of the Higher Worlds*, for otherwise you will only remember as far back as the point in childhood when the astral body had already united with the physical body in such a way that you can no longer distinguish between them. But if you develop this faculty you will be able to go back, remembering how as a very young infant you willed the whole physical body. And you then begin to grasp what we do after death, when memory has been taken away after just a few days. We then continually desire the physical body we had in the last life. And this takes longer.

It is something one can also try out. For if someone has reached the age of 60, let us say, and makes this inner experiment, remembering back to his childhood and there finding the astral body, he will get to know this astral body quite well. But he'll find that the process is very different now that he is 60 than it would have been if he had done the exercise ten years earlier. This changes with one's age. For it is easier to go back when you are 60 than it is with 50. And at the age of 25 one hardly manages to go back at all. At the age of 20 you can't go back at all to your astral body. This, then, is something that changes as life progresses.

It is thus possible to get to know the astral body, and you are then able to say: the astral body becomes different the older you get. The older you get, the more desires do you develop, and people therefore also have more desires if they have gone through death after reaching more of an age than if they are still very young. Then the human being has fewer desires. After death the human being will live in his astral body for as long as he has not learned no longer to desire his physical body. The next time we meet I'll show you why we have to say: man lives a third of his lifetime in the astral body after death, but only a few days in his ether body. There is not enough time to go into this today.

And then the human being will be completely free of all desires. He'll then no longer desire his physical body, and at this point something strange happens. He will no longer have the desire for the physical body which he had before, but he is given the possibility of making provisions for the physical body he will have in the future. And he then goes through a work process in the world of the spirit that will enable him to have a physical body again in his next life on earth. This takes the longest time of all. This is how he comes to have another life on earth again.

The next time we meet I'll show you that 'eternity', as we call it, can well be shown to be a reality. I'll bring the matter to a conclusion then. This has in fact been part of the question put to me.

But, gentlemen, the way I have explained the matter to you was to take you first of all, really, into the spiritual aspect. I told you that in addition to the physical body we also have an ether body, an astral body and an I. The I is already there before a human being is not just born but before he has entered into embryonic life, been conceived. It is there.

But you see there is a particular dogma of the Church that says something very strange. This was in fact soon after Christianity had spread.[23] In the dogma, the Roman Catholic Church forbids people to believe in life before life on earth. Why? You see, people do not concern themselves much with life before life on earth. They'll say: 'Well, I'm here. Life before this life is of no concern to me.' But life after death is something people are very much concerned with, for they do not want to stop being alive. This is of interest to people.

It is, however, impossible to learn about life after death if one does not always learn about life before birth, that is, before conception. The one is not possible without the other. So what happened when the dogma was established that one should not consider life before life on earth? People's view of the supersensible was cut off. But does it serve a purpose for the Church to cut off this view of the supersensible? Oh yes, it serves a purpose, for since human beings desire to have life after death, the Church is then able to make itself responsible for everything to do with death. People will not be able to know what happens after death, and have to depend on what the Church tells them. And this will make people long to believe above all in the Church. It was therefore a good thing—that is, for the Church—to establish the dogma that human beings go on living after their life on earth. For with this the Church took control of everything connected with death and dying.

I once had a talk with a famous astronomer.[24] He did not believe anything about anthroposophy. But it is true nevertheless that astronomers find it easiest to understand that we cannot stop at the physical world. We were talking about Church and State. His attitude to the two was that he rather liked the State, but liked the Church less, saying it guides people to mere faith and not insight. And he then put things rather well, saying that the Church has it easy, much easier than the State, for the State only has to control life, whilst the Church controls death and dying. And because it looks after death and dying, the Church has much more in its favour, has much more success.

The science of the spirit, anthroposophy, wants to help people realize that they have responsibility for their own dying. That is the thing. You see, gentlemen, that will mean real progress. People will then no longer just want to feel dependent, but to take their lives into their own hands. And that is what matters.

People are already aware today that things cannot go on the way they have done in the past. In the past they would think: 'I'll have to work for a time in my life, that has to be, for if one did not work, life could not go on; but afterwards I'll get my State retirement pension.' That was the general idea. And when I die, they would say, the Church will put my soul in retirement. You see, they then retire to enjoy eternal bliss, doing so without insight and without doing anything about it themselves.

Real progress will consist in people taking their lives into their own hands, not letting themselves be organized by State or Church, but getting somewhere by themselves, out of their own resources, insight and will. And for this they will need to have scientific understanding of their own immortality.

5 *Discussion of 21 March 1923*

Human life in sleep and death

Good morning, gentlemen! Let us try and bring the subject we have started to a conclusion, at least for the time being. You see, we only learn to understand life if we begin to consider the sleep of human beings, which I have mentioned to you a number of times before. When we are in the fullness of life from morning till night, we usually think that sleep will give us energy again, getting rid of the tiredness, and so on. But sleep actually does much more than that. Just think about it. Looking back on your life, think of the dreams you had in your sleep. These do not always come to mind. Dreams are something we soon forget, as you all know. Though perhaps once in a while you did have a dream that you would often tell. You remember it because of the telling. But the dreams we do not tell vanish in no time at all. Going back to the time when you were boys in your memories, you'll recall many things from your boyhood and from later on in life. But your memories are always interrupted. If you think back over today, you come to the time when you slept. That is a break, something you do not remember. Your memories only start again with last night, going back to yesterday morning. So that in remembering back we do not get the whole of our life, for the part that was during the night will always be missing. If you draw a line to show the process of remembering back, there is a period of time, from evening to morning, that is beyond recall; then you have recall again from morning to evening, a pause again from evening until morning, and so on [Fig. 16].

Our recall of life is really such that there is a whole part of

Fig. 16

our life which we do not remember. This is quite clear. It is the time we have slept through.

Let us now think of someone who is unable to sleep. As you know, many people complain of being unable to sleep. But many of those complaints should not be taken seriously, for some people will tell us they never sleep at night, and if you ask them for how long they have not been sleeping at night, they'll say: 'Oh, not for years!' Well, someone unable to sleep for such a long time would have been dead long since. People do sleep, but they have such lively dreams in their sleep that they feel they've been awake. Now tell such a person: 'Have a good lie-down, you don't need to go to sleep; just lie down.' For he'll then sleep all right, and though he may not know it, he does sleep. I just wanted to tell you this so that you can see that people really need sleep in their life. Sleep is more important for life than food is. And someone who would be unable to sleep would not live.

Well, now, how much time do we spend asleep between birth and death? You see, gentlemen, the sleeping time is longest for very young infants. When an infant is born he'll sleep almost all the time. Gradually the time spent sleeping grows less. And when you've reached something of an age and reckon it up, you'll have to say that you have really slept through one third of your life. And that is healthy. We really sleep through one third of our lives.

This has been known for a fairly long time. Only people don't like to remember things that have been known for a long time. Just as far back as the nineteenth century, right at the beginning of it, people writing about these things would say: 'Man should work for 8 hours, have 8 hours for himself and sleep for 8 hours. That gives us 16 waking hours and 8 hours of sleep, with 3 times 8 = 24 hours. And one third of the 24 hours is given to sleep.' This was a perfectly accurate observation. Man needs a third of his whole life for sleep. But of course people don't consider how important sleep is for life, for they do not care about soul and spirit today. They only concern themselves with the things they experience when their bodies are in the waking state, but not with their soul and spirit. And that is the way it is, so that people will often say in their everyday lives today: 'Lord, yes, it is a good thing to sleep, but all it needs is that you're tired enough.' And they'll then drink enough beer at night so that they'll be able to sleep. But it is not a matter of being tired enough; what matters is that people realize the real importance of sleep.

Let us clearly understand what it really means to sleep. You see, gentlemen, basically people like themselves a great deal. You see this especially when they are sick. Sick people show how much they like themselves, for they'll take very good care of themselves when they have a pain somewhere, and so on. All this is quite right and proper, but it does show that people are terribly fond of themselves. What is it they are fond of when they like themselves so much? They are fond of their bodies. And this is the great secret of life, I'd say, that people are fond of their bodies. And the love they have for their bodies shows itself when something is not quite right with their bodies.

But there's also a drawback to this fondness for the body. The body is active all day long. The body toils hard all day long. And the liking which the element of soul and spirit has for the body gets less and less as the day goes on, though the person is not aware of this. This is the strange thing, something we should know. During the day, when a person needs to be active all the time, the element of soul and spirit gets less and less fond of the body. That is why an infant sleeps such a lot. It loves its body very much, always wants to enjoy it. Looking at an infant you can always see how he enjoys his body. Just think of an infant who has had his milk and goes to sleep. In this sleep, the infant relishes his digestion. He enjoys the processes that occur in his body. And he'll only wake up again when he's hungry. For he is less fond of what happens when he's hungry. So he'll wake up again. You see, therefore, that an infant wants to enjoy his body in sleep. You can make the most wonderful observations. But the academics don't do this, for they do not have the ability.

Look at a herd of cows feeding in their pasture and then lying down contentedly to enjoy their digestive processes. They are enjoying the processes that happen in their bodies.

This is something we have to know — the human being really wants to enjoy his body. But it is a bit different with humans than it is with cows, and again a bit different with an adult than with a child. The young child is not yet working and therefore enjoys his body in sleep. The cows do it all from instinct, and therefore also enjoy their digestion in sleep. The human being never gets to enjoy his digestion. Using his body all day long he has reached a point by evening when he is quite out of sympathy with his body. He does not like it any more. And you see, that is why he sleeps. He sleeps because his body is no longer dear to him. The antipathy a person develops to his body all day long will make him go to sleep at night, and he'll sleep until he's overcome this antipathy in his soul, waking up again when he is once more in sympathy with his body. This is the first thing we need to understand, that waking up occurs when the individual is in sympathy with his body again. And this sympathy is for all the individual organs in the body. When someone wakes up, therefore, he slips into his organs, as it were.

Just think of the way waking-up dreams are. Our waking-up dreams are such that we may dream of snakes, for example. We are slipping into our intestines at that point and dreaming of snakes. The snakes represent our intestines.

The human being thus slips into his body with spirit and soul when he is in sympathy with his body and wakes up. He has to have this sympathy, otherwise he'd always want to leave his body.

And now consider this. Someone has died, he has put his body aside; the body is no longer part of the human being. The first thing to happen, as I've told you, is that he has thoughts that recall the whole of his life. And these thoughts are lost after just a few days. They disperse into the whole world. But he'll still feel sympathy for the things his body has experienced. And this sympathy will gradually have to go as well. This is the first thing we go through after death, that we must lose the sympathy we have with our body.

How long does it take for us to regain sympathy for the body when we live for one day? It takes a third of the day. And because of this, losing that sympathy after death also takes a third of our whole life. Someone who has lived, let us say, for about 30 years will need about 10 years to get rid of his whole body, so that he is no longer in sympathy with the world and with life—all this is approximate, of course. So a human being first has a few days after death when he recalls his life, and then he is weaned, I might say, from this backward look, which will continue for a third of his life span on earth. This is the average term for human beings, but it will be longer for some and shorter for others, for one person is more in sympathy with his body, likes himself more, and another likes himself less, and so on. After death we therefore go through something which we might describe as: 'The human being weans himself from all the things that connect him with his body.'

Now you may well say that the things I am telling you are

really quite theoretical. How can we know that a human being is still attached to something when he has put aside his physical body? How can we know that? Well, gentlemen, to know this we have to look at the way a human being develops in the course of life.

We have the first period in life in which the human being develops, the first period of time in life; it continues until the individual gets his second teeth. First he has his milk teeth, then he gets his second teeth. Now you see, we can say that the milk teeth are something we inherit. But the second teeth are not inherited. The second teeth come from the ether body. The ether body is active in us and gives us our second teeth. So we have the physical body, as I wrote it up for you the other day; this gives us our first teeth. Then there is the ether body; this gives human beings their second teeth, the teeth which remain.

Now we really must develop the ability to see. Today people only develop the ability to think, form theories, but not to see and behold the things I have described in my book *Knowledge of the Higher Worlds*. If we really look at a child who is gradually getting his second teeth, we see the ether body at work at a level not apparent to the ordinary senses. And this is the body which we keep for a few days after we die and which then disperses throughout the whole world. So if we make a real study of what gives people their second teeth, we find that after death human beings have their ether body for a few days and then cast it off after those few days; that is, the ether body goes out into the world.

Now we still have our astral body then and our I. The astral body is the part of us that goes on longing for the physical body. With the I, which is inside it, we continue to long for the physical body. We may say, therefore, that man develops needs and desires in his astral body — as I told you the other day. All needs are developed by the astral body.

They are not part of the physical body. When the physical body has become a corpse it no longer has any needs [Fig. 17].

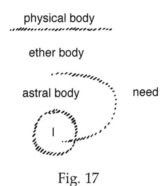

physical body

ether body

astral body   need

I

Fig. 17

Thus we are able to say that the principle which gives human beings their second teeth will also be gone a few days after death. So what remains? Here we must find a way to study what begins to be particularly active in the human being from the time when he has his second teeth to the time when he reaches sexual maturity. This is another important period in human life. These things cannot be studied in modern science where no attention is paid to them.

You see, from the getting of the second teeth to reaching puberty something is active in the child that is not perceptible to the ordinary senses. And what does this invisible principle want? It gradually wants to take hold of the whole body. It is not yet in it when the child has his second teeth and begins to receive this astral body into the whole of his body, so that it may be present in all parts of it. Then the child matures more and more. And when the astral body is wholly in the body the child has reached sexual maturity. It is important for us to know that it is the astral body which brings sexual maturity into the child.

It is, of course, not possible to study these things the way modern academics would like to study them. Modern academics only want to study the things they can lay their hands on. They do not observe human life. But anyone who has learned to observe properly what it is that works its way into the body from the second teeth to puberty knows that this is the astral body. This gives rise to all needs and desires. A child does of course have needs even before he gets his second teeth, at a time when the astral body is mainly present in the head; but later it spreads through the whole body. You can see very well how the astral body spreads if you look at boys. The voice changes as they reach puberty. This marks the astral body entering into the whole physical body. In women you can see it from the way the secondary organs of their sex life, the breasts, and so on, develop. This is the astral body entering into them. And human beings keep their astral body even when they have cast off their ether body after death.

How long has someone been in his physical body when he is 30 years of age? He's been in it for 20 years; for 10 years he was not in it. After death he wants to be in it again for those 10 years during which he was not in his physical body, which he has slept through. He will therefore be active in his astral body after death for one third of the life he has gone through here on earth. After this time, the astral body will be satisfied and the human being then lives only in his I. Having gone through about one third of his life span after death, the human being lives only in his I.

But this I, the truly spiritual element in man, will now need tremendously much to be able to live on. You see, it was not without reason that I have all the time told you that common sense, the rational mind, thoughts, are really spread out over the world. I have told you that everything in the world is really arranged in a sensible way, if one studies it properly. I have explained this to you by speaking of the animal world. This whole world is such that we should not imagine our own rational mind to be the only one; the rational mind we have has been taken from the rational mind spread out in the world — like a portion of something with a ladle. Rational thinking is all-present. And anyone who thinks his rational mind is the only one is as foolish as someone who thinks: 'I have a glass of water here. The glass was empty to begin with, then it was full, that is, the water has grown out of the glass.' No, the water must first be got from the well, from the whole body of water. And that is also how we first have to get our own thinking mind from the big rational mind that is in the world.

We simply fail to notice any of this in our lives. Why? Because it is something our body does. Gentlemen, if you were ever to know — I have spoken of this before — what your body does with a very small lump of sugar you have eaten, with the sugar not just dissolved in the body but transformed into all kinds of other substances — if you knew everything that was going on there you'd be amazed. You are amazed even when I tell you just the very beginnings of everything that goes on in the human body. But however much of it all you consider, you are always only considering a little bit. You take a breath. The breath you inhale must always be used in the whole of your body. Just think, you take a breath about 18 times a minute. And that breath you take must always be used in the whole of your body. That needs tremendous rational thinking, an absolutely tremendous rational mind.

Now our body does all this. Our body really works for us with tremendous good sense. It is truly admirable, and we have to feel this when we discover how much the human body really produces by way of good sense. It is simply enormous. Our body therefore relieves us of a great many things during life.

But now, after death, we no longer have it. Now we do not even have the ether body any more. We do not have the astral body, nor even a longing for the physical body. All we have, therefore, is the I, and the I now realizes that it does not have the body and begins to familiarize itself with everything that will be needed for a body.

And this is where something tremendous comes in, something we need to understand. In modern science things are made very easy in this respect. People will say: 'Where does the human being come from? Well, the human being comes from something that has arisen in the mother through fertilization, as a fertilized egg.' In modern science it is said, therefore, that you have the fertilized egg and inside it, well — somehow the whole human being is already laid down in there. Someone who knows nothing will say: 'A germ is there; the whole human being will come from this.' Now you see, people have got this really clear in their minds long since, but in their own way, which means they have got it really unclear.

Just imagine this is the egg [Fig. 18] from which you have come. So you would be in there, a tiny human being, as it were. But this egg has itself come from another egg. So this tiny human being must already have been in the maternal womb, and the maternal egg, that is, the mother herself, must have been inside the grandmother, and so on through great grandmother, great great grandmother and all the way to Eve. And you arrive at the strange notion that the whole of humanity was inside Eve, the original mother, but

encasement theory

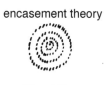

Fig. 18

one inside the other like a nest of boxes. Mr Müller was inside an egg; this in turn was inside an egg together with all other human eggs, only it was like a nest of boxes. The whole human race was inside Eve, the original mother. This thesis was called the theory of evolution at the time and later, derisively, the encasement theory.

From the beginning of the nineteenth century people said one really cannot imagine that the whole of the human race was encapsulated in Eve, with one always inside another, and so terribly many of them—this simply will not do. And they then accepted another theory. They then said: 'No, there is really nothing inside the egg; but when the egg is fertilized all the external conditions affect it—wind and weather and sun and light and all kinds of things. And the human being comes into existence under the influence of the whole natural world.'

Indeed, gentlemen, materialists feel really good with an idea like this. But it does not stand up to close scrutiny. For just imagine what becomes of us with the whole of nature having its effect on us all the time. It will make us nervy, as people call it today. Someone who is sensitive to every draught of air and every ray of light will not be a proper human being but a fidget. The natural world around us actually makes us fidgety. So that cannot be the answer.

Proper study actually shows us something completely different. Proper study shows that there is nothing at all in the egg. Before it is fertilized the situation is that one sort of discovers all kinds of things in it, I'd say. It has form. We are therefore able to notice all kinds of threads and so on in the unfertilized egg. But when the egg is fertilized the threads are destroyed and the whole egg is then nothing but a real scrunched-up mess, if I may put it like that. To put it in a more formal way, it is a chaos. It is matter lacking totally in organization.

You see, matter lacking completely in organization does

not exist anywhere else in the world. All forms of matter are somehow organized, inwardly structured in some way. If you take anything whatsoever, just a speck of dust, and look at it under the microscope you'll see how finely and beautifully it is structured inside. The fertilized egg is the only thing that is in utter chaos inside. And matter must first fall into utter chaos, it must not be anything in itself any more if a human being is to come out of it. People are always thinking about protein, for example. They always want to find out how it is organized inside. Well, protein has an inner structure for as long as it is not fertilized. Once it is fertilized it is what I've called a 'scrunched-up mess', meaning a chaos, absolutely disorganized matter. And the human being comes from this.

Even in the case of Eve, if she ever existed, there was no whole human race, not even later in a fertilized egg, for the egg is completely chaotic, lacking all order, and it also was without order in Eve, the prime mother. And if a human being is to arise from this egg, this must be brought about from the outside, that is, the human being must enter into this egg. Proper scientific study will indeed show that the human being must enter into the egg from outside. This means that the human being comes from the world of the spirit. He does not come out of matter, for matter must actually be destroyed first.

It is like this even with plants. There you have the soil, and the seed in the soil. Again people do not make a proper study of what happens with the seed in the soil. For the seed must first be destroyed. The next spring then makes the new plant rise from the destroyed matter in a spiritual way that comes from outside. It is like this with animals and above all also with man. It is only that the plant has it easier. The whole universe creates its form. With man, the whole universe does not create his form to begin with. He has to create it himself. Man actually just enters into this destroyed matter himself, otherwise it would not be possible for a human being to arise from this destroyed matter. Man must therefore first come out of the world of the spirit and enter into the destroyed matter. The whole of fertilization merely ensures that when a human being wants to come into the world he is presented with destroyed matter, that he has the destroyed matter. He would not be able to do anything with matter that was not destroyed. He cannot come into the world the way a plant does, for then he could only become a plant. He really must create the whole universe within himself. And he does create it. And that is a truly wonderful thing the way the human being configures the destroyed matter to create the universe in it.

Let me give you an example of how the human being configures the destroyed matter to create the universe in it. If this is the surface of the earth [drawing on the board] — we can do it like this, for if you look at just a small part of the earth it does look level. The sun rises in the morning, goes up to a certain height and then goes down again. This is a specific angle, with the sun rising that far. It is most interesting that the sun always rises up to a certain level and then goes down again. The angle is of course a little greater in summer than in winter, but the sun always rises to a specific degree. This angle therefore marks an inclination of the sun to the earth.

We also find this angle somewhere else. You see, when light enters into the eye, we have the blind spot, as it is called, at the point where the optic nerve coming from the brain enters into the eye. This is a spot where we do not see. We only see really clearly in places that are some distance away from this blind spot where the optic nerve comes in. And this is what is so interesting — the spot where we have the clearest visual perception inside us is at the same angle to the blind spot as the sun is to the earth in its orbit.

And there is something else as well. If you take the heart,

it is at a slight angle. It has the same inclination as the sun has to the earth. I could tell you any number of things that would show you how everything that exists out there in the universe is also inside us in some way. The inclination of the sun is something we have in the inclination in the eye and in the inclination of the heart. We are entirely created out of the good sense that prevails in the universe.

You know, gentlemen, this is something where one begins, as one gradually gains some insight, to say to oneself that man is really a whole small world. Everything which exists out there in the world is recreated within the human being.

Just think what it would be like if you were given this 'scrunched-up mess', this destroyed matter, and asked to recreate all those things in there. You would not be able to do it. You see, when the I is all by itself after death, it has to learn from the whole world how to recreate the whole world. Having cast off his sympathy with the body during that period of a third of his past life, the human being then begins to learn from the whole universe how to be a human being again. And this takes longer than a life does on earth, for the way things go on earth, well, you can learn a lot or learn a little. Most people really learn very little today. And strange as it may seem, the academics learn least of all, for the things they learn are all quite useless. They only make it possible to know what a corpse looks like, but not how a living body is inwardly brought about. But that is what the I has to learn after death. It must learn all the secrets, from the whole world, of how a living body is built. And there we may refer to this time which the I spends learning from the whole world how a human being functions and lives inwardly.

You see, if someone does the exercises I have described in *Knowledge of the Higher Worlds* and is then able to remember the time which one otherwise does not remember, the time when he was a very young infant, he will discover what the life of an infant consists of, an infant who knows nothing of the world as yet, but merely uses his body, merely wriggles, merely lives his way into his eyes, into his ears, but does not yet understand any of it. In ordinary life people do not generally look back. They'll say: 'Why bother about my infancy; I'm here, that's all.' But when one does look back into that short period which one usually does not remember, and does so with insight, one notices what one was actually doing then. And to begin with you get a terribly unpleasant feeling as you come to this. For the wriggling of the very young infant is an effort to forget all that knowledge of the universe. It is given over to the body, and the body will later know it. It will be able to take over that knowledge in its life.

The young infant gives his body the wisdom of a whole world. It is really most painful, terribly sad, that in modern science people have not the least idea of what goes on in the life process, with the young infant giving the universal wisdom it has gained to his body, and gradually growing into his eyes, into his hands. He gradually grows into them, giving the whole wisdom of the I over to the body. Before that, the I really held the whole wisdom of the world.

It may perhaps seem strange to you, but it is really so: how is it possible for someone who truly has anthroposophy — knowledge of the human being — to tell people something about the universe? One is able to tell something about the universe simply because one is remembering one's earliest childhood, early infancy, when one still knew the whole of it, having learned it earlier, before having entered into the body. And anthroposophy really consists in gradually rediscovering this whole universal wisdom again from the body, to which it has been given.

Yes, gentlemen, we are not shown how to do this in modern science. It does not tell us at all how we can regain the knowledge which we ourselves have put into the body in the first place. In science, people are shown how to experiment, and to learn only the things they can learn from this in a superficial way. The right thing would be to take the human being into the living body. Our students are taken to a dead body, a body that is already a corpse, and they do not learn anything about the living human being. It would, of course, be more difficult to do this, for it needs people to practise self-knowledge, looking inside themselves, for there the human being is meant to grow more perfect. But this is exactly what present-day people do not want. They do not want to be more perfect, they want to be drilled a bit in their education, and stop at that; they do not want to be more perfect. People do not want this because with the education they are given today they are already too arrogant, I'd say, to admit that there is any room for improvement.

So I have now told you a little bit, for the time being, about the I. But we'll talk more about these things in the next few sessions, so that you will hear a great deal more and gradually find it easier to understand it all.

You see, I've told you a little bit about what the I needs to do during the time before the human being comes down to earth again. There are people, however, who'll say: 'Really, I am not interested in what the I needs to do afterwards. Surely one can wait until one has died and then see for oneself.' That's what people say.

Well, gentlemen, that would be the same as if the germ, having developed and been fertilized, with the human being now inside it in the maternal womb, were to say: 'Oh, I find it too boring to live in the womb, I'll leave early.' But it will not be a human being unless it spends the allotted nine months in the womb. This is something it must first go through. In the same way the I will not be able to gain living experience after death unless it lives in such a way here on

earth that it is encouraged to do so. It is therefore quite
wrong for someone to say: 'I'll wait until after death; then
I'll no doubt see if I am something or not,' and so on. People
really aren't very logical. They are about as logical today as
the man who insisted, who swore that he'd not accept any
god. He swore: 'As sure as there is a god in heaven I am an
atheist!'[25] That is more or less the way people are today.
They use the old turns of phrase even if they are contradictory. And so they think they can wait and see if they still
exist then or not. You see, people say to themselves: 'Do I
believe in immortality or do I not believe in immortality?
Well, if I do not believe in immortality and it exists after all,
I might fare badly. But if I do believe in immortality and
there is none, no harm will be done. It is therefore definitely
better to believe in immortality.'

But I think you'll agree that we must not play games with
our thoughts like that. It is important to be really clear in
one's mind. And so we have to say: 'The human being must
receive the stimulus he needs here on earth so that his I may
really penetrate into the world in a living way after death.
And this stimulus is thoroughly driven out in modern
science, where people are not made in the least aware of the
facts as they really are. It is something that is not admitted,
but it is really considered a good idea to keep people as
unknowing as possible today, so that they'll sleep after
death and have no idea at all of how to penetrate the secrets
of the whole universe, and thus be truly human again.

You see, gentlemen, if humanity were to go on living the
way people live today, being concerned only with superficial things, people will be born at a future time who will
not be able to lift a finger, having learnt nothing before their
next life.

The way lives follow one another is something we'll come
back to another time. Today I only wanted to give you ideas
so that you may see that I was not careless in my use of

words when I spoke of the way the I is after death, for it is possible to show, from the knowledge itself, that the human being comes down to earth again and has to create his life for himself in that chaos of matter. This is genuine knowledge based on objective facts.

So this is what it is all about. Only it can't be done so quickly, but I am still going to answer the question fully for you, taking all the things together which we know about the end of human life, how the human being gradually loses his ether body and his astral body, and how the I must then come down to create its astral body and so on. That is what it is all about, how man comes down to earth again and again. And in time one then also discovers when the human being will be freed from the whole of earth life and no longer needs to come down. The question as to when he originally started is one we'll also answer in due course. He must have started at some point as a kind of plant. He did not need to be human for this. But I have also spoken to you of the time when the whole earth was one large plant, and we shall see that one day the earth will be a plant again, and man will then be free from being human.

I'll then consider the whole matter once more from another aspect. You will, of course, have to be patient and not say 'I can't follow this' when we are only just starting. You'll see, the more we go into detail the more it will seem plausible to you.

Essential human nature — physical body, ether body, astral body and I

Gentlemen! In modern science, only the things one can see with one's eyes, touch with one's hands are accepted. It needs an extra faculty to explore the things one cannot see with one's eyes, touch with one's hands, and people are not willing to work so that they may gain this faculty. Medieval knowledge based on faith meant that people had knowledge, a science, of all things that are of the earth, and they had a dogma of faith in what is written in scripture. People still hold this view today. They no longer want to venture beyond and gain knowledge that cannot be immediately apparent, for they have not really gone beyond a science of things that are tangible. I'd like to explain what I have been saying a little bit more by speaking of something that is quite old in present-day terms. But the really important developments relating to the subject actually came in the last third of the nineteenth century. All I have to do is to read to you the last sentences in a book and you'll see right away how modern scientists think in this respect. It says: 'There is nothing that will take us beyond the boundaries of our knowledge. We can only let ourselves be taken into the trackless ... [gap in shorthand notes] sustained by unceasing hope in a sweet, mystic semi-asleep state, on the wings of our imagination,'[26] and so on.

So what the gentleman is saying is that things have to be tangible; then we have science. The rest is a figment of the imagination. Everyone can pretend this to himself and have others pretend it for him; it is fantasy, for we simply cannot know anything about it. And if people take comfort in all kinds of supersensible things, well, we need not deprive them of this.

It is really terrible to see the confusion that has arisen about this. Now, however, I'll show you how these gentlemen have literally forgotten how to think with this science of theirs. I'll demonstrate this to you by referring to another passage in the same book. For what does this gentleman—who says everything we cannot touch is a matter of belief—do? He says it is nonsense, scientifically speaking, to think of an eternal I living in the human being, for the I is merely the sum total of everything else we have in us. We are in the habit of taking everything we think and feel, from beginning to end, together and consider it a single whole. And having made it a whole we call it our 'I'. That is what the gentleman says.

He then wants to illustrate this. He wants to show that we do truly bring everything we experience in life together and call it our 'I'. For in that case 'I' is just a word, as we are simply putting it all together. He then offers an analogy. He compares everything the human being experiences in life with an army, a company of soldiers. And so everything I have known in my youth, as a child—the way I played, the feelings I had when playing—is one group of soldiers; the things I came across a bit later are another group of soldiers, and so on. I then gather up everything there has been to this day, just as soldiers are brought together in a company, and call it 'I'. That is what he says. He therefore compares all the individual inner experiences we have had with a company of soldiers, and makes them a group the way we put things in groups, not saying Miller and Tennant and so on, but 'No. 12 company' and so on. He thus gathers up all the inner experiences of the I in a company of soldiers. And he goes on to say: 'On the other hand there is something else to be said about the I, for it must also be taken into account that from the time of life when conscious awareness has to some extent developed, one always feels oneself to be the same "I", the same person.' What he is saying, therefore, is that we must finally get people out of the habit of feeling themselves to be an I and get them used to the idea that this is no more than as if one is gathering together a company of soldiers.

'Seen from our point of view, this should not really be particularly surprising. In the first place, we must be clear in our minds, if we want to consider this more closely, about the way we should really consider the individual person in relation to the outside world.' So he first of all tells us nicely that we should form an idea. And his answer is: 'It is the result of all kinds of individual ideas, and above all ideas that bring the direct interactions between the organism and the outside world together in a more or less compact whole. In our view, the idea of the I is no more than an abstract idea of the highest order, built on the sum of all the thinking, feeling and will a person has, and more than anything all ideas concerning interrelationships between one's own body and the outside world. The term brings all this together, just as the term "plant world" encompasses the infinite sum of all plants. The word "I" ' — this is where it gets interesting — 'is the representative of all these ideas, more or less the way the leader of an army represents all the individual soldiers. Just as we can say of the actions of an army leader that in the minds of individual soldiers and units within the army he provides the bedrock, more or less darkly and unconsciously, exactly so do a mass of individual concrete ideas and feelings provide the basis, the bedrock, for the term "I".'

Well now, gentlemen, just consider the way the man is thinking. It is a very learned book, we have to recognize this, at the highest level of science. The man says that we have a company of soldiers and the leader of the army. But only the soldiers are taken all together; the leader is merely their representative. And the same is said of ideas and feelings. All thoughts and feelings are taken together, with the I merely their representative.

But you see, if the I is the representative, if it is a mere word, then in the case of a company of soldiers the leader of the army must also be regarded as a mere word. Have you ever known a case where the leader of the army, the man leading a company of soldiers, is just a word, a word put together from all the individuals? Well, we might imagine that the leader of the army is not particularly bright. Sometimes the I, too, is not particularly bright. But to imagine that the leader of the army is nothing but a word — and this is the analogy he uses for the way the I relates to our ideas — simply proves that even the cleverest of people turn into blockheads when they are supposed to say anything about things that are not apparent to the senses. For as you have seen, we are able to show that when they produce an analogy it is completely without logic. There's no logic there at all.

Having produced his nice analogy, the gentleman went on to say: 'This shows that the concept "I" always depends entirely on the basic idea someone has. It can be seen most clearly as it gradually develops in a child. But every thinking adult person can also establish for himself that he feels himself to be a different I now than he did ten years ago.'

So let me ask Mr Erbsmehl or Mr Burle if you feel yourself to be a completely different I than you were ten years ago! I am sure you are able to tell if you are someone quite different now than you were ten years ago! But you come across such passages wherever you look in books today. The most ordinary facts of everyday life are turned upside down. It is of course complete nonsense for someone to say he feels himself to be a different I than he did ten years ago. But that is what those gentlemen say. But the moment you start to think about the I, if it is the same today as it was ten years ago, you no longer find, you are no longer able to say, that the I dies when the corpse dies. The question is why?

I have spoken to you, gentlemen, about the way you cut your nails, the way your skin flakes off, and so on. All this happens over a period of seven or eight years. Today you no longer have a particle in you of the matter you had ten years ago. For as your skin flakes off, your inner part is all the time moving away from the body. You see, your body is like this. At the top it flakes off; then the next layer moves up and flakes off in turn; then the next one moves up, flakes off, and after seven or eight years it has all flaked off. Where is it? Where is the body you had ten years ago? It has gone the same way, only in a rather more complicated way, as the dead body does when it is put in the grave. The dead body becomes part of the earth. If you were to split the dead body up into particles as small as the skin flakes you are losing all the time, or the nails which you cut off, if you were to divide it up into such small particles, you would not notice either that the dead body goes to some place or other. One might blow it away. And that is how the physical body becomes part of the outside world over a period of seven or eight years.

But if you still feel yourself to be an I today, and your physical body died two or three years ago, then the I simply has nothing to do with the physical body, the way we have it there. But, you see, it does have so much to do with it that if you pick up a piece of chalk, you will say: 'I've picked up a piece of chalk.' Everybody says that. I had a school mate — I think I have told you this before — who was well on the way to becoming a proper materialist when he was about 19 or 20 years old. We used to go for walks together, and he would always say: 'It seems perfectly clear to me. We don't have an I, we only have a brain. The brain does the thinking.' And I'd always say to him: 'But look, you say *I* go, you even say: *I* am thinking. So why are you lying? To be really honest, you would have to say: My *brain* is thinking!' Perhaps one should not even say 'my', for 'my' refers to an I; surely there has to be an I if one says 'my'. People never say: 'My brain is thinking, my brain is walking, my brain picks up the chalk.' They wouldn't dream of it, for a human being cannot be a materialist in life. He would talk nonsense the moment he became a materialist.

But people cook up materialism in theory and do not consider that genuine science does in fact know that we no longer have the body today that we had eight or ten years ago, so that the I has remained. And you are also able to remember back to your early childhood, to your second, third, fourth, fifth year. You would not dream of saying that it is not the same I which then ran about as a little boy. But let us assume you have now reached the age of 40; going back to your thirty-third year you lost one body, back to your twenty-sixth year another, back to your nineteenth year a third, then a fourth back to your twelfth and a fifth back to your fifth year. You have lost five bodies and your I has always been the same. This I therefore continues for the whole of your life on earth.

The I is also able to do things with your body. It can all the time direct this body which it is losing. You see, when I walk, my legs, though quite old, are really only six or seven years old where their substance is concerned. But I control them with the old I that was there even when I ran about as a little boy. The I is still walking about. The I controls the body during life on earth.

Now I have told you that a child learns to walk, talk and think in the time which we are no longer able to remember. We cannot recall the times, of course, when we were not yet able to think. We learn to walk, to move about altogether, to use our bodies, to talk and to think. It is something we learn. And one has to control the body in that way. When you are crawling about on all fours as a young child you cannot make the body come upright unless you have the will. When you move your hand the I says: 'I am moving the hand' — the I with its will. And that is also what happens when the child has the will to come upright. The child learns to talk with the will. The child learns to think with the will. And so we have to ask: How come that the child learns all these things? And we discover that although the body is continually replaced in the course of life on earth, the I always remains the same; this I is still the same by the time we have learned to think, to talk and to walk. This I was already active in the body at that earlier time.

Gentlemen, I have shown you how one really gets one's body. You see, scientists think — I already explained this the last time: 'Ah well, one simply gets one's body from one's mother, one's father. Then it is all prepared, and one is already a small human being. We inherit it; the body is something we inherit.' Well, a science where it is said that we inherit the body really is not worth the powder to shoot with. For you only have to look at a bone — here you'll need to remember some of the things I told you before — if you look at a thigh bone, for example, you find it a wonderful sight. Such a thigh bone has a whole scaffolding structure. The scaffolding in the Goetheanum was nothing compared to the beautiful scaffolding one can see in the whole of this thigh bone if one looks at it under a microscope — a marvellous structure, handsomely built [Fig. 19].

If you cut off the tip of your nose — it only needs to be a very little piece, of course, for it would not be healthy to cut off too much, but one could cut off just so much that it does no harm. Looking at it under the microscope you again see a marvellous structure, most handsomely built. Yes, gentlemen, you have no idea how beautiful the tiniest part from the tip of your nose really is! Admirably well designed. And that is how it is with every part of the human body. It is

Fig. 19

handsomely built, perfectly arranged. The best of all sculptors could not do better.

There is only one part in the human organism where everything must be destroyed, so that there is nothing but matter—I referred to this the last time. This happens in the egg from which the human being develops. And with fertilization we have the last act; form or design is removed from matter.

We are therefore able to say that the bone is beautiful; every single thing is beautiful. The tip of the nose is not as beautiful as the bone but it is still most handsome. But the egg, from which the human being will later arise, contains nothing but matter in complete chaos, for in there everything is shattered. It is all atom, and there is no form in there at all. Why?

A human soul cannot simply enter into a bone. Superstitious people sometimes think there is a little devil somewhere in their bones or limbs. Well, figuratively speaking that may sometimes be true, but a human being certainly cannot enter into such a bone. Nor can a human being enter into the tip of your nose.

I did know a lady once who insisted she had the holy spirit in her left index finger, and she'd always consult it if she wanted to know anything. She'd do so if she thought of going for a walk, and so on. But that's nonsense, of course, superstition. What we have to say is that no human being, no human soul, no human spirit can enter directly into such a well-designed bone, nor into the tip of one's nose. The thing is like this. The human soul and spirit, the I itself, can only enter into the egg because there matter is nothing but dust, world dust. And what happens is that the soul then works on that world dust with the powers it has brought with it from the world of the spirit.

If people believe that a person simply comes from a father and a mother by means of heredity, then one has to assume that there is a tiny human being there. But that goes against scientific knowledge. Scientific knowledge tells us that the protein in the egg is reduced to dust. And the soul, coming from the world of the spirit, from a world that is beyond sensory perception, actually builds the human body out of this protein that has been reduced to dust.

Now you may ask why a child looks like his father or his mother. Well, gentlemen, that is because the child always goes on imitating. Someone who says: 'He is the spitting image of his father' could also put it differently. You see— let us wait a while with the child—let us say we have a child who looks very much like his father or his mother, though in fact it is not all that marked. Children grow much more similar later on than they are when they are very small. But of course such things are of no interest to the learned gentlemen. But let us wait a while and not form an opinion when the child is only one or two weeks old, or a month; let us wait until the child is three or four years old. He will have started to talk then. Someone comes along and says: 'Amazing. The father is German, the child is also starting to talk German; he must have got it from his father; he's inherited it from his father, for his father is German. This is quite amazing! Since the child has come from the fertilized egg, the language must have been there already in the egg. It is only surprising that the child was not able to talk when he came from the egg, from his mother's womb.' But I think you'll agree that the child did not inherit his speech at all, he acquired it by imitating others. His speech is similar to that of his father and mother. But no one would dream of saying the child inherited his speech.

In the same way the face is similar. But why is the face similar? Because the soul, when it lets itself be born by a mother or begotten by a father, who is Mr Miller, makes the face similar to that of the father or mother, just as the child will later make his speech like that of his father and mother. This is something you have to consider. The child develops the sounds, the words of his language by making himself similar to his parents or the people who bring him up. But earlier than that the soul is unconsciously working like a sculptor on the face, or the gait, and so on. And the similarity arises because the child has been born into the family and makes himself resemble them when he does not yet have conscious awareness. This happens in the same way as the similar way of talking develops.

You see, gentlemen, in this way we discover that the human being does indeed come from the world of the spirit, the world not perceptible to the senses, and builds his own body with all its similarities. Just look at an infant. The infant is born. Sometimes it is not easy to distinguish children from little animals when they are newly born, though their mothers will, of course, find them most beautiful. You see, people are little animals when they are born—compared to later on, of course. They are really quite unattractive, those infants. But the soul element is gradually working things out in there, making it all similar, more and more similar, to a human being, until the moment comes when the infant learns to walk, which means he finds his balance on earth, as I told you the last time. Then the child learns to talk. He learns to use the organs in his chest, for these organs are located in the chest. Then he learns to think, meaning he learns to use the organs in his head.

So let us consider this. The child learns to walk, which is to keep his balance and to move. What does he learn when he learns to walk? He learns to use his limbs as he walks. But we cannot use our limbs without at the same time also using our metabolism. The metabolism is connected with the limbs. Walking, keeping one's balance, moving has to do with the metabolism and the limbs.

Then the child learns to talk. What does this mean? Talking has to do with the organs in the chest, with breathing. The child has been able to breathe even as a young infant. But to connect words with the air he pushes out, that is something the child learns with the organs in his chest. Keeping one's balance is therefore connected with the limbs, talking with the chest, and thinking with the head, the nerves.

And now we have three elements that make up the human being. Just consider this, three aspects. In the first place we have our limbs and metabolism, in the second place a chest, and thirdly our thinking, the head. We have three aspects of the human being.

1	{ walking keeping balance moving }	limbs metabolism
2	talking	chest
3	thinking	head (nerves)

Now let us take a look at the child. It is like this with a child. When he is born he differs from an adult not only in the way he looks — the cheeks are different, the whole form; the forehead looks different; I think you'll agree the child looks different. Inside, however, he is even more different. The brain mass is more like a brain mush in the infant. And up to the seventh year, up to the time when the child gets his second teeth, this mush, this brain mush, is made into something truly marvellous. From the seventh year onwards the human brain is quite marvellously structured. The soul, the spirit has done this inside; the element of soul and spirit has done this inside.

But you see, gentlemen, we would be unable to shape and develop this brain in such a marvellous way up to our seventh year if we were not all the time in touch with the world. If you have a child who is born blind, for instance, you'll immediately see that the nerves of vision and with them a whole part of the brain remain a kind of mush. This is not beautifully developed. When someone is born deaf, the nerves of hearing, nerves that come from the ear and cross here [drawing on the board], after which they go over there, remain a piece of brain mush along this way. It is therefore only because we have the senses that we are able to develop our brain properly in the first seven years of life.

But the brain does not develop anything for you that you might reach out and touch. You could of course stuff tangible materials up your nose, if you like, and into the brain—you would ruin your brain with this, but it would not lead to anything. All the matter we can reach and touch therefore does not help you to develop the brain in the first seven years. It needs the most subtle forms of matter, like the subtle matter that lives in light, for example. Ether is what is needed.

You see, this is most important. We absorb the ether through all our senses. So what is it that develops all this activity coming from the head? The activity that comes from the head and also extends to the rest of the child's organism does not come from the physical body. The physical body is not active in the marvellous development of the child's brain; it is the ether body which is active. The ether body, of which I have told you that we still have it for two or three days after we die, is at work in the child. It makes the human being develop a perfect brain and thus become a thinking human being. We are therefore able to say that the ether body is active in our thinking.

With this we have once again found the first super-sensible aspect of the human being — the ether body. A child would not be able to develop his brain, he would not be able to have a human brain in him, if he were not able to work with the ether body that is all around. Later on in life we can strengthen our muscles by making them work, by physical, tangible methods. But the left parietal lobe of the brain, let us say, to take an example, cannot be strengthened by any physical or tangible means. To make the muscle stronger you could use a weight and lift it again and again, over-coming gravity. But you have to use a material, tangible thing to strengthen the muscles. Just as you have your biceps muscle here, and are able to strengthen it by lifting and lowering weights, in the same way you have here, looking at the head from the front [Fig. 20], a brain lobe. It hangs there just as the arm hangs here. You can't attach weights to it. All the same, there is simply no comparison between what happens when you develop a muscle and what goes on in this brain lobe. At first, when we come into the world, it is mushy; when we are seven years old it has been marvellously shaped and developed. Just as the muscle in your arm is strengthened by lifting and lowering the weight, which is something tangible, getting stronger because of something we are able to see, so the brain is

Fig. 20

strengthened by something that is in the ether. Man relates to the whole world around him through his physical body, and he also relates to the whole world around him through his ether body. And that is where he gets his thinking. With this, he develops the inner parts of the head in the first seven years.

When someone has developed the power of thinking he comes back again, I would say, to speech. Learning to talk is something very different from learning to think. Learning to think is a process that shapes and develops our body. It makes us into sculptors, I'd say, this thinking. It is working in us so that by our seventh year we shall be complete human beings. We also learn to talk during this time. But you see, it is not possible for us to learn to talk the way we learn to think. For when we talk — what happens? Well, gentlemen, you see, if you lift a heavy weight, or hit out strongly with your arm, the arm will hurt. To hurt means to have sensation. We really have a sensation when we use one of our limbs to excess and so injure it a little bit in some way. If you have a pain it always means that something has been injured, even if only just a little bit. You then have a sensation, you feel something. But you know, gentlemen, the whole of our speech comes from our feeling. If you listen to a child you can hear how speech comes from the realm of feeling. The child will learn soft sounds *ei, ei* [German sounds, pronounced i, i in English] in his language. What does he want to bring to expression by saying those sounds? He is cuddling up. He likes the person against whom he's cuddling up. He rests his little head as he makes those sounds. And that is how it is with all words, with everything that is uttered — it arises from something we feel. Now feelings do not come from the brain, nor do they come from the element that shapes and develops the brain.

You see, if there were no sunlight coming in through our eyes, the ether that is all around us would not be able to work on us. We would not be able to bring ourselves to full expression in those first seven years. A child also has basically just feelings in the first seven years. He learns to talk by imitating others. But there is feeling, the way he feels, in this imitating process. And we have to say that light cannot call forth feelings. When we learn to talk through feeling, something else is active in us. The principle that is active in speech, through which human beings are able to talk, is not just the ether body, it is the human astral body. We are therefore able to say that as a second principle we have the astral body in us for learning to talk — astral body is just a term, I could also use another word. We have the astral body which is above all active in the chest, in our breathing, and then transforms itself as we learn to talk.

You see, people always think human beings are hungry or thirsty in their physical bodies. But that is nonsense. Think of a machine driven by water. You have to give that machine water. All right, it'll run then, and if you do not give it any water it'll stop running. What does it mean when we say the machine has stopped running? It means you have to give it more water, you have to give it a drink. But the machine did not feel thirsty. The machine does not get thirsty; it will stop, but it does not get thirsty first, otherwise it would scream. It does not do so. It does not feel thirst.

So how is the situation in the human being? When a child is thirsty he does not behave like a machine. He does not simply stop. Quite the contrary, he'll start to roar most powerfully when he's thirsty. So what is the connection between being thirsty and screaming? The screaming is not based on matter, nor on the ether. The ether can give form and structure; it is therefore able to create our form. But the ether does not make us scream. If the ether were to make us scream there would be a terrible — well, not perhaps roaring, but a continual hissing in the world. For when we look at things it is the ether which together with our eye makes us see. The ether is all the time entering into the eye. And that is why we see. Yes, but when the ether comes into the eye, it does not go z-z-z-el in the eye; you know, that is not the human ether body, for it does not lisp. Just think if just from the fact that we are looking there were to be a continuous whispering in an auditorium—that would be a fine thing! The ether body does not scream, therefore, nor does it whisper. Something else is there. And that is the astral body. And when an infant is thirsty and cries, the feeling of thirst is in the astral body. And the crying lets the infant's feeling reach our ear.

But everything I have been describing to you would still not make me able to walk. For, you see, when I create my body with the ether body, coming from the head, I might be a statue for the whole of my life. My body might be created, I might roar like a lion; my roar might always be created in a process that comes from the astral body. But if I want to gain my balance as a child, if I want to use the will, therefore, so that I may walk, take hold of things, gain my balance—all things where I say 'I walk, I take, I gain my balance'—then the I is coming in as well, and this is a little different from the ether body and the astral body. And this I lives in my limbs and metabolism. When you move your limbs, that is the I. So you have three aspects of the human being, apart from the physical body. You have the ether body, the astral body and the I.

$$\underset{\text{astral body}\quad 2\qquad\quad}{\underset{}{}} $$

I	1	{ walking keeping balance moving }	limbs metabolism
astral body	2	talking	chest
ether body	3	thinking	head (nerves)

And you see, these three aspects of the body can be perceived if we first train ourselves for this. But in modern science people do not want such training. And I am now going to tell you how people behave in modern science who do not want to do this.

I am sure you've all had dreams on occasion. Whilst you are dreaming you believe it all to be reality. Sometimes you wake up in a dreadful state of fear, because you are standing on a precipice, get giddy and fall down, for example. You wake up dripping with sweat. Why? Because you thought the precipice was real. You are in bed, lying there quietly, there is absolutely no danger, but you wake up because of the danger you've been facing in the dream image. Just think, if you were to sleep all your life—that would be a nice thing for some. There are people who sleep all through life.

There was someone once who had studied Copernican theory. He was a terribly lazy chap. So one day he was lying in a roadside ditch. Another fellow came walking along and said: 'Why are you lying there?' 'Because I have so much to do!' 'Come on, you aren't doing a thing!' And he said: 'I have to move with the earth's orbit around the sun, and I want to stay behind. It's too much of an effort for me, too much to do!'

You know, some people don't even want to move with the earth around the sun. But we do go along with the whole of our waking life. You see, if we were to dream all our lives, we might lie in bed in Europe, say; someone would pick up our body—perhaps with the bed, so that he won't wake us—and take it to America on a boat. It would, of course, need angels to do this, for people cannot do it that surreptitiously, but it would be possible to transport us to America. There we would dream on, and anything might be done with us; we would know nothing about ourselves. Dreaming there, we'd never know how the nose feels to the touch, how the left hand feels when taken hold of by the right. And yet, gentlemen, we'd have a whole life. If we were to dream for the whole of life, it would be something different—we might be able to fly in our dream, for example. Only the fact is that on earth we cannot fly; in our dream we fly. We would think ourselves to be quite different creatures, and so on.

But just consider, there would be a world all around us as we dreamt our way through life. And we do, of course, wake up. Let us say I wake up and I have been dreaming that during the night—let me take a promising example—I was hung by the neck or beheaded. Let us assume someone dreams he's been beheaded. It would not be as great a cause for concern for one as it would be here. One might perhaps have it happen on several occasions that one dreams one is beheaded and one would believe that this did no harm. Now you wake up—and lo and behold, you had taken a book to bed with you and that has come to lie behind your back as you turned over. So now your head is lying on the edge of the book, which is uncomfortable, and in your dreams this makes you think you have been beheaded. Once you're awake again you realize what the dream meant; after waking up you can discover where the dream has come from.

So we must first of all wake up. Waking up is what matters. For people who dreamed all their life their dream world would be their only reality. We only begin to take our dream world for a fantasy world when we wake up.

Well now, gentlemen, a person wakes up in bed of his own accord or because the world around him shakes him awake. But it needs a special effort to wake up from the life in which we are, the life where we think the only things that exist are those we can grab hold of. And how to do this, how to wake up, that is something I have described in my book *Knowledge of the Higher Worlds.*[27] Just as we wake from a dream and know that the dream is a world which is brought about by the waking state, so we wake from our waking state when we gain higher insight and know that our ordinary world comes from the things we perceive in that higher waking state. It is something one knows.

In future, therefore, science must develop so that we do not just dream on in the world, always only trying to see how one may do things in the laboratory, in the physics cabinet. It must show people how to wake up. Then people will no longer say: 'Man is only a physical, material body' but 'Man consists of physical matter, of the ether body, astral body and I.' And of these one would then be able to say: 'We now know the part of the dead body that is a waking-up part, even when we die.' For the ether body first had to come to the physical body and shape and create the physical body using the head. The astral body had to come, first had to dig itself in a little in the chest, and then the person learned to talk. And the I had to come to the physical body and get it in balance in the outside world. The body then learned to move its limbs and adapt its metabolism to the movements. Man thus brings his ether body, his astral body and his I from the world of the spirit, and the chaotic matter which has been reduced to dust he shapes for himself, using the ether body, astral body and I. And these things, which he brings with him into the world, he will take with him again after death. I have already given you some indication of how that goes. So the situation is that if one really takes up this higher science, this waking-up science, one is able to speak just as well about life after death and before life on earth as one is able to speak about this life on earth. This is something we'll do the next time. Then the question as to what the human being is like when he has no body, which is before fertilization, will have been fully answered.

The next talk will be at 9 o'clock on Monday. The subject is a bit difficult at the moment, but that does not matter. The reason for it being difficult is merely that people are never prepared for these things when they are young. If they were prepared they would not find it so difficult. Today, I would say, people have to make great efforts to learn the things at a later stage for which no preparation was given when they were young. But when you see that people actually go so far as to say, 'The leader of the army is only the sum total of a company of soldiers,' you will also see that modern science certainly needs to be improved. And this, then, is something which really enables us to understand the things that are not perceptible to the senses.

Dream, death and reincarnation

We'll now try and continue our discussion of the things we have been considering these days. I have been telling you in more general terms how this element of spirit and soul in man relates to life in the physical world perceptible to the senses. Today, I'd like to take this further. I have told you before that if we want to know something about these things it will not do to say: 'The rational mind, and after all I have one, must decide everything, and anything it cannot decide does not exist.' We really have to remember that we have gone through a process of development even in ordinary life. Just think what it would be like if we had remained at the level of a three-year-old child! We would see the world in a very different way. A three-year old sees the world very differently from the way an adult does. The three-year old lets himself be taught all kinds of things. He is really still asleep as far as ordinary life is concerned. A three-year-old cannot even talk properly; he is learning the language. And a three-year-old is altogether modest and not arrogant. He allows himself to be taught. He probably would not be so modest if he were not half asleep, other-wise he'd say: 'Why learn? We know it all already!' That is what people say today: 'We know it all already, and since we have no insight into things of spirit and soul with our rational mind they simply do not exist.'

Now if I were a three-year-old child and I were to say: 'I don't want to learn anything else. It's enough for me to say daddy and mummy and a few other things — apple puree and so on,' that would be a child's point of view. But even when we have acquired the usual rational mind we still have something in us that can be developed further. And if we develop the ordinary powers of insight that we have, taking them further, we will be able to make another leap, I'd say, like that from young child to adult person. All this does of course depend on gaining the insight, and basically speaking it should already be part of the whole of human education. Today people cannot help themselves but be arrogant and say: 'I know it all, and anything I do not know is no concern of mine.' A person cannot help but say that because from when he first started school he has been taught in such a way that he put everything down to the rational mind, which he possesses, and says that anything else may be something you can believe in, but you cannot know it.

You see, we have to be very clear in our minds that there really is such a waking up from ordinary everyday life to real knowledge, just as there is a waking up from being asleep and dreaming to ordinary life. You simply have to realize that one can really only know something about the world if one takes a higher point of view and is able to see through the things that happen, just as we have to see through a dream from the waking point of view. For it is only then that we'll know that the dream was not reality, but something that depended on our waking life. This is when we can come awake. I told you the other day: if we were never able to come awake we would believe the things we dream to be the only reality.

But let us look and see now what a dream really is. You see, gentlemen, people have given a great deal of thought to dreams. But everything people say about dreams is really a kind of drivel, fundamentally speaking. It is really a kind of drivel, for people are able to say: 'Well, when the brain starts to oscillate just a little the person will dream. Yes, but why does the brain oscillate just a little?' So the things people say about dreaming are really just a way of proving things. But if you are clear in your mind that human beings have not only this physical body [drawing on the board] which we see and are able to touch in life, but that they also have the other aspects of which I have spoken, that the human being also has an ether body, an astral body and an I, and if you then say to yourself that this I and this astral body are outside the physical body and the ether body during sleep, you'll in the first place be able to realize why a person does not walk in his sleep. He does not walk because the I is not in the physical body. You can also realize why a young infant does not walk. Because the I has not yet woken up in the young infant. So you are able to see why a person walks. He walks because the I slips into his physical body. You can also see why people do not think in their sleep. They do not think because the astral body is not in their physical body.

So you see, this shows that we must distinguish, as it were, between physical body and ether body—lying in bed—and I and astral body, which are outside during sleep.

Now just think what it is like when you wake up or go to sleep. When you go to sleep the situation is that the I and the astral body are just departing. So there will also be a stage where they are still half inside as they go out. The stage where they are completely outside, the I and the astral body, will only come after this. But there is also a stage where they are half inside and half outside. Then we dream.

People usually think we dream during the night. In actual fact we only dream on going to sleep and on waking up. And what do we dream? Well you see, gentlemen, people think we dream because we use the brain when we are awake—this is what today's academics say—and only use the spinal marrow when we are asleep. That is what they think.

But these people are simply not able to observe things! Take a real dream. Take the dream of a fire, for example.

You dream of a great 'fire; you dream of all kinds of things. And as you wake up, someone is shouting 'Fire, fire' outside. In reality therefore all you took note of—you did not know anything about the fire and so on—but because the ear is open then, you just half heard this shout of 'Fire, fire!' Being in the habit of it you connect this with the fire, but only rather darkly. And your dream of fire may be about something quite different than anything you will then see. You may dream, for instance, that the fire is due to a volcanic eruption. You may dream something completely different. And when you dream of something that happened to you years ago, you know how confused the dream will be. Maybe you had a minor dispute with another boy in your young days. Now, years afterwards, you dream about this. But in your dream it is as if you were killed, or as if you killed the other boy. The dream throws everything into confusion. And this is something you'll always find with dreams—they throw everything into confusion.

Now when we dream as we go to sleep the matter remains in confusion. When we dream as we wake up it will be corrected, for we actually see the situation as it is. We have dreamt someone was murdering us. He put a gag into our mouth and then came and belaboured us with some instrument or other. We wake up and find that we've suffered the mishap of getting a corner of the bedcovers in our mouth.

You see, the dream takes a minor thing to set it off, adds a great deal to it and creates confusion. If the air is bad in the room where you're sleeping, you may suffer a nightmare, as it is called. But you don't say to yourself in your dream: 'The air is bad, I can't get a good sleep,' but have the impression of an evil spirit sitting on your chest and causing pressure. You know the tales and legends about this. Nightmares arise when we get bad air into our lungs.

How do dreams arise?

Well, gentlemen, let us take a waking-up dream. The I and the astral body are just slipping in and have not yet fully come in. These are the dreams we are most familiar with. When you are completely inside your physical body you look out through your eyes. But when you are not yet quite inside, you do not look out through your eyes. You have to see it like this: once you are entering into the physical body you turn round, as it were, and look out through your eyes. But when you are still half outside you go through the eyes, slip through the eyes, and then you see nothing clearly. You then develop all kinds of confused fantasies. But that is all we have, when we enter into the body after our night's sleep—these confused notions. And how do we actually put them to rights? We don't put them to rights. Our body puts them to rights for us. Otherwise we'd always see Vesuvius spewing fire every time we heard someone shout 'Fire!' outside. Our eyes are so marvellously organized that it is only by looking through them that we see things rightly. If we were out of our bodies for the whole of our lives we'd be given up to all kinds of fantastic things all our lives. The body actually makes it possible for us to see life in the right way.

So you see, when we look at ourselves as we are out of the body we are in reality inwardly in our I and in our soul; we are divorced from reality, creating all kinds of confused ideas in our I which must always be put to rights in our body as we wake up every morning. It is thanks to our body that we see things properly. We are in fact dreamers, divorced from reality, in our life on earth. The dream shows us how we truly are in life on earth.

If you come to gain real insight into things because at a later time you woke up in a particular way where your insight and perceptions are concerned, you will come to realize that during life on earth man is what he dreams. He is really fantasizing, and always has to have himself put to rights by his body. And when he is wholly asleep he is really quite powerless. In that case he cannot perceive anything of the world. It is only when he has a little bit of his body that he perceives the world in fantasies.

But it is exactly when one knows this that one says to oneself: 'What is a dream, really? What does a dream actually show me?' The dream shows us that we really know nothing of our body; for if we did know we would also be able to see the outside world properly. We might recreate our eyes in mind and spirit. But we cannot really do it; we have to depend on the body giving us the power of the eyes. The dream thus shows us how little we know of our body.

Now you'll remember my telling you the other day that we have to create this body for ourselves. Heredity is nothing. What we have when a human being begins existence on earth is matter that has fallen into dust. I have told you of this. The element of spirit and soul must enter into this. The human being must first build up his whole material substance for himself. If he understands the nature of dreams he knows that he cannot do this. And when we come to see through the nature of dreams we also discover something else.

Consider how hard it is to go back to our childhood years in our minds. Suddenly an event comes to mind where we know: 'This is something my mother did not tell me; it is something I saw for myself.' This will have been in the third year for some people, in the fourth year for others, and so on. Yes, gentlemen, until then one was asleep, really asleep. But when you look at such a three-year-old who is really still able to sleep—for one does not remember this time, just as we do not remember the times of ordinary sleep—if you look at this child in relation to life you find he can do something which we cannot do in later life.

As I told you, the brain is finely developed up to the

changing of the teeth, up to the seventh year. Look at the brain of a newborn infant and the brain of a seven-year-old. Something has been going on in this child, something has been working on that brain. The brain itself cannot do anything. The brain is like a dynamo. A dynamo develops magnetism and the running of the whole factory depends on this dynamo. But first an electric current must pass through, otherwise the dynamo won't work. The brain won't work unless the current of soul life passes through it. That current of soul life is much more powerful in the child, for up to the changing of the teeth the child is developing the whole of his brain, and he does so most of all in the earliest years of life. This is why I told you about Jean Paul, a very clever man, saying: 'One learns a lot more in the first three years of life than in three years at university.'[28] The work one has to do there is much more skilful than anything one will ever have to work on in the world later on.

So there one says to oneself: 'Yes, that is something we had; we have lost it. This inner work of the soul was lost at the very time when we gained conscious awareness. We no longer have it.' And when one comes to realize this one will know that one is less and less able to do it. Gaining the ability later on to look back into life, one begins to feel quite funny seeing everything that has been going on. For when one was a boy of 14 one was perhaps still able to do a little of the vast abundance of things one had been able to do at three or immediately after one was born. Then one was able to do most. At 14 one was already able to do very much less. And when one is 30 one has just enough left to be able to digest things — but one can no longer develop them. By 50 or 60 one has become quite an ass where the work of developing the human body is concerned. And one then realizes how much of an ass one becomes as life on earth continues. It is necessary for us to discover that having lived for 20 or 30 years one loses some of one's wisdom. Having lived for 30 or 40 years one has lost a great deal more. And after that one is a terrible ass with regard to all the things one should be working through inwardly.

But if one begins to gain insight, acquiring the ability to look back into life, it really makes one feel great respect for the clever creature one was as a very young infant. You may have been terribly ugly then; but you were able to change everything, if you were an ugly chap. At 15 one can no longer make oneself handsome. As a young infant one can do just that. All young infants can do it.

It is therefore important to realize what an ass one has become in the course of life. That is an important aspect of life. You therefore do not grow immodest but become a truly humble person. And if you gain the right insight you'll realize: 'As a young child you really sat on the ass and drove the ass yourself. Now, having grown old, you have become the ass.' You see, it has to be put in such strong words, or we'll simply get nowhere.

And this is also the way of discovering the nature of dreams. You'll have known this yourselves — in your dreams you may actually think yourself to be the Emperor of China or anything you like. There are many other kinds of dreams. You may dream all kinds of things. But what does the dream show us? Here we must pursue the dream to see how it changes in the course of life on earth.

The dreams of young infants are quite marvellous. Infants' dreams still show that the child has the powers in him to shape and develop his body. They are truly cosmic. The child dreams of the things he experienced before he came down to earth because these powers are still in him. He needs them to develop his brain. When you have this marvellously crafted brain which is in the uppermost part of the skull [Fig. 21] — the eye is here, and the nerves he needs in order to see are here. All this has to be worked out in fine detail. He has to work it out in fine detail. Yes,

Fig. 21

gentlemen, this is something you cannot work out on the basis of earthly knowledge. You can use earthly knowledge to develop machines here and there; but you cannot use earthly knowledge to develop the brain. And looking at the dreams of young infants one can see exactly that they have the way of developing their brain in their dreams. Later the dreams will also become very peculiar if someone does not lead a well-ordered life; they will increasingly fall into disorder. And a dream is full of confusion because one knows so little of one's physical body, because one is not inside it.

The reason that we know so little of our physical bodies is that the wisdom we were given when we came down into life on earth has gradually been lost in the course of life, having changed into soul quality. Waking up and saying to yourself, 'Well, if you believe all the things you have been dreaming—that you are the Emperor of China,' you are certainly an ass. But we ourselves cannot do anything but develop ass qualities, for we do not have the body. Not being inside it, we cannot help but be confused by the dream. We have completely lost the ability to develop the body in the right way, an ability we had as young children. The body has to come to us from outside. When we wake up it comes to us from outside. But when we come down to this earth again, it will not come to us from the outside. Instead matter that has been destroyed will meet us in the egg, and we'll have to build it up piece by piece.

All these are things we have to learn between two lives on earth. Between two lives on earth we have to learn what the dreaming human being can come to be. You see, some people who are hostile to anthroposophy and oppose it say: 'These people just want to dream; they come up with all kinds of fantastic ideas about the world.' Ah, but anthroposophy actually means that we no longer attach importance to dreams, for dreams show that we are not able to do the things we were able to do with the dim, unconscious knowledge we had when we entered into this world as little children. We therefore understand clearly that we gained this ability in a world that is not the world here on earth, for here we can only become divorced from reality as regards our true I. Beautiful as this world may be, we can only be divorced from reality in it where knowledge of our real I is concerned. The relationship we have to the body, the whole relationship to the body, is something we have to gain in another world.

Now let me tell you that someone who is able to see through it all and therefore also realizes that this process of becoming an ass goes on and on will know that it is easy to lose that knowledge. You see, it is very much the same as when we take an exam. When someone has to take an exam he will often swot for two years and then just as quickly, terribly quickly, forget it again. And that is how it is with the knowledge we need to develop our bodies—we soon forget it. Only the 'quickly' is a bit different from the way it is with exams. It goes on for our whole life on earth. When we have died, we have more or less forgotten what we took down into physical life with us at our birth. Our lifetime is more or less the time of our forgetting.

Now imagine that one of you has a memory: 'That was

me, a growing child; the first thing I remembered was, let us say, something when I was four years old.' Let us assume someone is 60 now, and at the age of 60 recalls an event that happened when he was just four years old. He needed 56 years after those four to forget, inwardly to forget. For 56 years his forgetting grew stronger and stronger. He spent 56 years becoming more and more of an ass. How many more times did he need to forget the things he still had up to his fourth year? Well, he needed as many times more as 4 goes into 56: he has needed 14 times his earliest childhood in order to forget. Having reached the age of 60 he will need 14 times as long again to regain the things he has forgotten in the world of the spirit. That will be 60 times 14 years, 840 years. After that he will have regained the ability to have the things the child had in his first four years to build the body. He will therefore be able to come back to this earth after 840 years.

One can only make such calculations, the way I have just written it on the board for you, in a responsible way if one clearly understands that it is like this if one is able to check what lies in our dreams, the way dreams take us further and further away from the world of the spirit.

And you see, if someone goes about and at a particular time is not at all able to enter into his physical body, he is a medium. Someone who enters into his physical body at the right time and uses it again — well now, that is a normal person. But when someone is all the time walking about in a state where the I has not entered into the physical body — you can even walk about in your sleep, you can talk when you walk in your sleep or lie in your bed — we need not be surprised at this; for if we throw a billiard ball and everything is level, it will roll on of its own accord. And so if someone is not quite healthy, when everything passes easily, his body not having the right degree of firmness, then the activity which normally is in the conscious mind can still continue to act. Such a person will be an automaton, however. A sleepwalker is not a human being but an automaton. And someone talking in his sleep does not say anything human. Just try it. You'll hear the daftest things when someone talks in his sleep, for he becomes an automaton, his I and his soul not being in his body.

But when this is only half-way the case and the person is only half an automaton—the entering process is such that the human being enters from the posterior part of the brain, moving forward—when someone only comes in half-way, he can close his eyes and, because the optic nerves are back there [Fig. 21, right] he perceives something, but it is something fantastic. And he may then also tell one all kinds of fantastic things, for, you see, he is not seeing but getting images. The hearing is located there, and the sense of speech there [drawing]. So he will also be able to talk away. Mediums talk, but they are not in this world. Because of this we cannot say anything mediums tell us counts, for they are only half-way in their physical bodies. It does not count at all. They are merely saying things which the human being perceives in his ass quality—a term I have to go on using here.

I have of course also heard of mediums who say magnificent things. It is true. Mediums will sometimes say magnificent things; but this need not surprise us. For, you see, if a major earthquake occurs somewhere, for example, the animals will leave the place beforehand. The humans will stay and allow the earthquake to destroy them. Animals are prophetic by nature, for there is rational sense everywhere; they have not yet stuffed themselves with sense. A medium is thus something that goes down to the level of the animal. It can say marvellous things, even making them into verse more beautiful than Goethe's verse—well, you see, because he goes down to the animal level of rational sense.

The opposite is the case for someone who is to gain

insight in the anthroposophical way. He must not merely come in half-way, as in his dreams, but must know everything the way another person knows it, and in addition also know the things one is able to know when one wakes up a second time. When you wake up this second time you get an idea of how this is. You say to yourself: 'Yes, if you have done something in your life on earth to get to know the human being, this will help you after death.' You will then find it easier after death to get to know the human body again. What one has to learn between death and the next birth is the inner nature of the human body. And you really have to understand that it takes a great deal to get to know the world. Students get in a fair sweat when they have to learn all about the outside world, learn to calculate how the stars move in their orbits, and so on, what the earth looked like when today's crayfish did not yet exist, and so on. There is much to learn. Yes, but the things we have to learn about everything outside the human being here on earth are nothing compared to the things we have to learn about the inner human being.

You'll say: 'But people do learn about the inner human being when someone has died; then they learn everything. They cut him up small, the human being, and learn from the corpse what the human being looks like inside.' But that's a very different thing. All the knowledge you're able to gain from a dead body will never enable you to produce a living human being. Yes, of course, for that you have to have conception. But the human being who has done his learning in the world of the spirit between death and the next birth is actually involved in his conception. On earth, we can only gain insight into things that are dead. We cannot gain insight into something that lives, let alone something that is sentient and thinks.

I would not have dared to write up these figures for you if it were not the case that on gaining higher insight one sees that the human being moves further and further away from the world of the spirit in the course of his life on earth. As a child—let us assume he dies at the age of 16—yes, then it will be different when he remembers back to his fourth year. He may die at 16 perhaps, remember back over 12 years, which is 3 times 4, and if he has lived to the age of 16 he therefore will really only need 48 years before he appears again. It is truly the case that one can reduce this to a calculation.

But something very remarkable shows itself here, gentlemen. It is this. As you know, the patriarchal age has always been said to be 72 years. When someone has reached the age of 72, the years that follow are really a gift. So you see [writing it up], that is the patriarchal age of 72. Let us assume such a patriarch to be a truly excellent person, as indeed they were in earlier times. Today we are so inattentive that we recall little of our childhood years. But those earlier people would remember back to their third or second year. And so they would have had 70 years to forget the child's wisdom, the higher wisdom. That means 35 times 2. In the world of the spirit, they, remembering back much further than we do today, would go through a period of 35 times 72 years, which is over 2000 years.

You see, if you observe the sun in the spring, it now rises in the constellation of the Fishes. In earlier times it would have risen in the constellation of the Ram, and our calendars today still show the Ram as the point where it rises. Which is not true, however. The sun rose in the constellation of the Ram until the fifteenth century. At that time it was right to say: the sun rises in the constellation of the Ram. Astronomers have grown lazy since then and go on saying the same, though the sun certainly no longer rises in the constellation of the Ram today but in the Fishes.

Now assume the constellation of the Fishes to be a certain size. There are twelve such constellations. When the sun comes up again the following year, it will be somewhere in the constellation of the Fishes on 21 March, as I said. And if you observe it the year after, it will have moved a little bit further, no longer rising in the same place; the year before it was a bit further back, again not in the same place as the other year [drawing on the board]. The sun needs a certain period of time to pass through the constellation. First it was quite at the beginning of the Fishes, and a time will come when it will come to the end of the Fishes. It will then have moved on so far that it will no longer come up in the Fishes but in the Water Carrier. At present, therefore, it is passing through the Fishes, later it will go through the Water Carrier constellation, still later the Goat, and so on. The sun takes about as long to pass through one such constellation as a human being who has grown very old will need on average to come back again.

So it means a great deal that the sun moves on from one constellation to the next. In my *Occult Science*[30] I showed first of all that the return of the human being has to do with the sun's movements. And we may therefore assume— science also shows it—that when human beings die today, they get the knowledge they need to build their bodies up again under the influence of the Fishes. And they will return when they can no longer learn anything from the Fishes but have to learn from the Water Carrier. And then they have to learn from the Goat. Then again from the Archer. And then they will come again when they have to learn from the Scorpion. And again when they need to learn from the Scales; then from the Virgin, then the Lion, then Cancer, then the Twins, the Bull and the Ram. Then they are back again at the beginning. And of course they will have learned a great deal by then. They will have gone the whole cycle once in 25,815 years, going through something like 12 earth lives, 11 or 12 earth lives. Now someone may say: 'All right, you tell us that human beings learn the things they need on earth, each time from a different constellation, a constellation that looks quite different.' If you look up to the Fishes, they look very different from the Water Carrier, for example, or the Goat, and so on.

But just think of having been here 800, 1000, 1500, 2000 years ago, let us say. Things would have been very different on earth then and you would have lived quite a different life. Maybe you would have been a contented farmer with a very small farm, a nice round belly and utterly contented. Now you are in the industrial workers' movement. That is something you have learned from the Fishes. At that earlier time, when you had grown your nice little round belly and been a contented farmer, this would have been something you had learned from the Ram. And so people learn the things they go through on earth from the very constellations.

You see, we can now say that the human being gradually gets around. If you have been here in 825 BC, for instance, in the ninth century, you would have been that round-bellied farmer. Now you have returned under the influence of the Fishes. But if you go all the way round and have come full cycle after 25,815 years, you will have learned so much in the meantime that you'll not need to be what you have been before, for you will then be at a much higher level as a human being. So we have to say to ourselves: After 25,815 years, when we are about to go down to the earth again, we shall no longer need to go down to the earth in this way, for we shall have learned everything there is to learn in this constellation.

And you see, there we come to something I have spoken of before. People who have studied geology in a very learned modern way will tell us: '25 million years ago things were like this and this on earth.' The question is, how do these people know that the earth was a body of fluid 25 million years ago? I have spoken of similar things to you before, but not such long periods of time. How do they know?

They will study the Niagara Falls, for instance. The water drops down over rocks. They will remove some of the rock over which it has run and calculate how much of it is worn away by the water in a year. Considering that so and so much is washed away in a year, they would then work out how far the rock must have extended when the water had not yet cooled down to be water but existed as vapour. And that is how they arrive at those 25 million years.

Now that is just as if I were to examine someone's heart. Today is the 9th of April. If we examine the heart today and then again in a month's time, it will have changed a little; then, another month later, it will have changed a bit more. And taking these small changes we work out what the heart was like 300 years ago. Fine, but it did not exist then. The calculation is correct, but the object did not yet exist. And that is how it is with the way the earth looked 25 million years ago. The calculation is perfectly correct, but the earth did not yet exist. And they also do calculations as to what the earth will be like in 25 million years' time. They merely go in the other direction for this. But the earth will no longer exist then. Just as with a heart, which is a little bit less good day after day, it is possible to work out what it will be like in 300 years, except that you'll not be here as a physical human being in 300 years' time. The sums are correct. People are blinded, deceived by the fact that their calculations are terribly correct; but the human being does not last as long as the time given in the sums. When you come back again after 25,815 years the earth will have dissolved in the meantime. You will altogether have been forced to discover in your consecutive lives that you have to find your way in the world in a different way. Then the earth will no longer exist; you'll be free of it. You'll have advanced to a higher form of life.

And by going into the matter in the right way we can be quite scientific and go as far as a time of which ancient legends still tell us, saying that man will still need to go through a number of lives on earth, and then he'll no longer need to come back to earth. He must then have learned enough to be able to manage without getting a physical body. By then, however, the human being must gradually have reached a point where he no longer has the crazy dreams we have today, and altogether no longer goes so far away from the world of the spirit.

All this will give you a very important result, gentlemen. For you have to say to yourselves: people who struggle against getting to know the world of the spirit do not want that wisdom to come to humanity. They want people to go on being asses on earth, and unable to go back. For by having gained some knowledge whilst still on earth about the human being, something living and not just knowledge based on the dead body, the human being also grows progressively more able to have a real insight after death into what he has to go through there.

If human beings, since they have after all to be asses on earth, were to remain asses, which is what certain shady characters want, these shady characters will cause him to lose his spiritual existence altogether. They talk to him of eternal bliss. But in doing so they take away from him what he has been given. This is something that has to be said; it is a terrible thing.

Anthroposophy is therefore needed to show human beings that they are truly able to gain insight and thus also able to enter into the world of the spirit again. This is the truth, you see, and anthroposophy does indeed have an important mission and great social significance for humanity. For the whole of the rational mind will go. And when people want to hold on to the rational mind by merely offering the human science that comes from the dead body, the outcome must be what has already happened: humanity living in such darkness that they simply do not know what to do. To get away from organizing all those eternal congresses, for example, and other such things, and make real progress, the human being must really be woken up. But people hate having to wake up. For you see, when people sit around conference tables it is not a matter of just sitting together but also of talking sense. But the way people are today they will not admit that they need to wake up first and make their minds a bit more flexible, so that they may also get inner feelings again about the social question. This is why basically speaking everything is just a patching-up job. What is needed is that people truly come to perceive and understand their inner nature whilst still on this earth, so that they will be prepared for the work they will have to do in the world of the spirit. That is indeed how it is.

Anthroposophy has nothing to do with converting individual people. Individuals cannot do anything, but many people can. The purpose of anthroposophy is to help many people gain real knowledge. Then it will in fact be possible to work for better times on earth.

This was something I also wanted to say to you, gentlemen. I'll have to go to Zurich, St Gallen and Winterthur now. When I'm back I'll continue with these talks. Perhaps you'll think of some things you want to ask me about in the meantime.

A symptomatic view of the astral body

I'd like to start today by telling you a story that is quite interesting. There were witnesses, so it cannot be said to be untrue. A gentlemen was fishing, using a rod, and after some time got annoyed because he had not had a bite. Then suddenly there was a tremendous jolt. Something really heavy had taken the bait. He pulled up his rod and was really pleased to have caught a big fish. But what did he land? A very large turtle.

This large turtle had swallowed the hook. It was in its stomach and the angler could not get it out. The turtle pulled in its head a bit more. First he tried to persuade the creature with kind words to let go of the hook. But it would not budge. So he had no other choice but this: he held the turtle by the tail, cut off its head with a sharp knife and let it drop.

Now you'll all admit that if this had happened to a person — let us say during the French Revolution or with any other instance of beheading — well, that person would have been dead. What did the turtle do? It got up on its legs, calmly marched back into the water and disappeared. It did not bother it in the least to have had its head cut off.

You see from this that for a time at least, the turtle did not need its head to go on living. The question as to how long it continued to live was not considered at the time, but you can certainly see that the turtle simply did not need its head for such things as walking, for instance. It is able to walk without having a head.

I have told you many stories of animals doing all kinds of things, terribly sensible things, and you can conclude from this story of the turtle that the creatures certainly do not do this with their heads. You can cut off a turtle's head and it will go on performing its movements and everything else quite properly. The turtle also did not run away blindly but straight back into the water from which it had come. It could not have done better if it still had a head.

Now you might say that this was an isolated case. But it was not an isolated case, for experiments of this kind have been done. Someone able to see these things in the spirit will not need such experiments. But they are being done all the time, in order to prove the matter wrong. They do not prove it wrong, however, but actually confirm it. The experiments about which I am going to tell you have been done countless times. You take a frog and cut off its head using a cut-throat razor. The frog is now without its head. You put it back on the table. It will first of all behave in an extraordinarily impertinent way without its head. It will go down a little bit in front and then most impertinently raise its hind part and hop away. If you now take an acid that burns and put a little on the frog's side here [drawing on the board]—this is the headless frog, these are its legs, only it does not have a head—so if you wet it a little with a cor-rosive acid, which normally hurts, the frog will first of all scratch itself using a hind leg, the headless frog. You can repeat this over and over again—the frog will scratch itself there, though it has no head. And if you use a bit more acid it will use its foreleg as well. This will make it go down on that side, of course. It'll topple over. So you see, a frog without a head does everything it would normally do and it makes no difference if it has a head or not.

Now of course you realize from this that when we go below the level of the mammals, to the lower animals, these lower animals will properly do without a head what human beings and higher mammals do with their heads on.

Now we need to see the situation very clearly. It proves

something. It proves that we do not need a head for things like these where we have a pain somewhere and lift a hand to rub the place. This is something a frog can do without a head. And so it is proven that this can be done without a head. So we certainly do not have a head in order to scratch ourselves. We do not have heads so that we may walk or run. A turtle or frog will walk without a head. So we do not need a head at all in order to walk. We can't quite do what it says in the fable of lazy Francis who was too lazy to walk but very keen on eating. You know the story. Then someone suggested he should walk with his gob and eat with his feet, so that he'd acquire a new habit. That's impossible, of course, but the situation is that we simply do not need a head in order to walk. Nor do we need it to move our hands.

So why do human beings and the higher animals need a head? What is the difference—now with regard to the head—between humans and higher animals on the one hand and lower animals on the other? The difference is that higher animals and humans die if they do not have their heads, but frogs, turtles and all lower animals live on. If you take even lower animals, worms for example—you can cut them in half and each half will walk by itself. So you see we simply do not need a head for the things which the body is really doing. The bad thing is, of course, that as a higher animal or human being one does need a head in order to live. And because we need it in order to live, we'll die when we no longer have it. It is not that we'll no longer rub away acid put on us if we don't have a head, but that we die without a head. A human being will no longer rub away the acid when his head is cut off. A human being would have behaved differently if he had swallowed the hook and his head had been cut off. Things would have been different even before that, of course, than they were with the turtle.

So we are able to say that in higher animals and humans,

everything connected with the head has nothing at all to do with the movements we make. All we owe to the head is that we live. When we no longer have it, we simply no longer live. Life is therefore in the head for the higher animals. In the lower animals life is in all the individual members of the body.

Let me now tell you something else from which you'll be able to see that there is also a big difference between higher animals and human beings when it comes to everything belonging to this head and this whole organization.

I am sure you have had experience of a children's disease that is a bit unpleasant. It is called whooping cough. It is not really all that bad for the child at the time when it happens, for he will normally get well again. The bad thing is that something remains if people don't do the right things — meaning doctors or whoever is responsible at the time — when a child has whooping cough. For then the following may happen. What does whooping cough involve? Whooping cough means that breathing in will always be as it should be — you may have a child with really severe whooping cough, it will breathe in properly. This can be seen if one studies the situation. But when the air wants to come out as the child breathes out it gets stuck, it will not come out the way it should, and then a bout of coughing develops. And with the air not getting out properly, fresh air cannot get in, and this causes the whooping cough. That is what it is.

But what lies behind it, when a child gets whooping cough? You see, what lies behind it is that the inner mucous membrane of the breathing system, of these tubes that go down to the lung and then out again, grows terribly sensitive. When the air goes in it passes over those sensitive places, for the chest is empty, and you can always pour air into something that is empty. Just think of a vacuum pump. A vacuum pump is a bell jar like this [drawing on the board]; you pump out the air and it is empty. You can have an opening to help you to begin with. If you take out the stopper, the air rushes in with a whistle. So there need be nothing but a vacuum under the bell jar. When we have breathed out our air, we have a vacuum in our lungs, and the air will rush in all by itself. You don't have to do anything special to get the air in. It is not surprising then that air will also rush in through a sensitive windpipe and sensitive tubes, for the air does not feel it. But when you want to get the air out of your vacuum pump again you have to do something, you have to pump it out. In the same way you have to push the air out from the lungs. But the child's breathing tubes have grown sensitive. They are just as sensitive as any other place where you may have got a scratch. The inside of the breathing tubes has grown a bit scratchy, and they are sensitive. The will impulse that pushes the air out will not do this but instead scratch away at the windpipe or tubes, getting involved with the scratchiness in the pipe rather than with pushing out the air. You see, wanting to scratch the child forgets to push out the air, and the air stays put in there. You then get these bouts of whooping cough. The body wants to push out the air by force, whilst in life it is the part of us which I called the astral body the other day that pushes out the air. Looking at a child with whooping cough you can see exactly where the physical body is and where the astral body is. When the child is not coughing, the astral body pushes out the air; the body does not have any problems at all. When the child has whooping cough, you have a sensitive spot there. The astral body wants to scratch away; then the physical body has to come in and push the air out forcibly, in spasms. This may even cause spasms, and then another disease may develop in consequence.

So you see it is simply not the case that we can say the physical body does everything. Otherwise we'll never understand whooping cough. When someone has got whooping cough, you have to develop a strange idea. You have to ask yourself: 'What has actually happened to his astral body?' His astral body has grown headless, just like the other part of the astral body in the frog! Just as the frog rubs away with its leg, so does the astral body inwardly rub away on the windpipe or tubes, and the physical body then has to come in to get rid of the air. So we can make a very clear distinction.

Now you may well ask me to prove it to you that the astral body, which is the soul principle, is actually involved in this case. Well, let me tell you what can happen when a child has whooping cough, with those sensitive areas in its air pipes, and the astral body wants to brush it away all the time, so that the child gets these spasms. Now imagine the parents bought a cat whilst the child had whooping cough, or maybe a cat had adopted the family—I am telling you something that is quite common. Whilst the child had whooping cough the parents bought a cat or a dog. This has made the child sensitive to the air the dog or cat had been breathing out. He would not have grown sensitive to this if he had not happened to have this sensitive spot at the time. Now, during the whooping cough, he has become sensitive. The child then recovers from his whooping cough, but sometimes a strange thing remains behind. If the child has not been used to having a cat around before, and a cat has come to live in the house whilst the child had whooping cough—this will not happen when he has just recovered, but later on the condition will develop which people call asthma, a breathing difficulty that repeats itself over and over again.

Now when this breathing difficulty comes—asthma always comes periodically, it comes and it goes—you may investigate it and you will sometimes find something strange. So a man develops asthma, for instance, and to begin with no one knows where it comes from. If you observe carefully you find that he gets a further asthma attack if there is a cat near him or in the room. If the cat is removed the asthma stops. There, you see, he is given a reminder, and he does not need his head for this. He need not even know that the cat is in the room. The cat may be in the room, he may not know it, but he'll still have an asthma attack.

And I can tell you about an even more magnificent case that is most peculiar. There was a child once who got this kind of whooping cough and, during the time when he had this, a lot a buckwheat was eaten in that family. This made the child particularly sensitive to buckwheat and he got a tendency, a talent you might say, to have asthma every time there was buckwheat in the room, or even just in the house. And then something very strange happened on one occasion when he was already a grown-up boy, a medical student. He lived on the top floor. The kitchen was down below, on the lowest floor, two floors lower down. On one occasion the boy upstairs got asthma, terrible asthma. He had only had it like this before if there was buckwheat in the house. They were very unhappy about this. Their cooks had always been told never to cook anything with buckwheat in it. It should never come into the house at all. What had happened? A new cook had come who did not know this. She had had some buckwheat down below on the ground floor, and the young student up on the second floor developed asthma. These things seem like fables. But they are completely true.

You will now also understand that human health and sickness is altogether connected with the whole environment. Thus it is not immaterial for our health if there are rats somewhere near or not. You see, the story of the cats I told you is so well known — human air organs having a particular sensitivity to cats — that it is actually called 'cat asthma' by the medical profession. You can find the term in their medical books. This is the kind of asthma people get if there are cats around. There are, of course, many kinds of asthma.

But the situation really is such that one has to say: having a dog or a cat or even buckwheat around is quite a commonplace thing for people. It merely makes an impression on the soul principle. But if the soul principle is not in order somewhere, the impression made on the soul principle remains quite unconscious. What has actually happened to someone who gets cat asthma or buckwheat asthma?

Well, whooping cough can be cured as follows. Let us assume a child has a sensitive windpipe or tubes; coal dust may have irritated them in some way. This may immediately cause whooping cough to develop. Such things can come from the tiniest little things. So the child's air pipes are irritated. What happens when such an injury exists in some place in the body? Well, you can see it if you cut yourself. If your body were just physical it would not hurt. Imagine you put on some really thick mittens. You can shape the mitten to be just like a skin. You can cut into it and it won't hurt. But why does your hand hurt if you cut it? You see, your hand will hurt because apart from a physical body there is also an astral body in there. The astral body is used to being in there. If you make a cut in the physical body, the astral body, which you can't cut, suddenly notices: 'Wow, there's no physical body there! That does not fit! It hurts.' You see, only the part which is astral body can hurt. It will hurt until the cut has healed up again.

And so the situation is that when there is an injury somewhere the astral body is left to itself. It gets out of the physical body.

Now imagine you get this fissure, this crack, in there in the windpipe or tubes; the astral body then comes a little bit free there. And the condition can be healed like this, if one does it very carefully. Let us say we have a child with whooping cough. We first of all put him to bed and let him get into a sweat – you can observe the whole thing step by step – he'll get really hot. The astral body easily joins with heat; it does not easily join with cold. If you let the child run around out of doors or even just indoors, the astral body can't get at the physical body because the warmth it needs is not there. But if you wrap up the child really warm – people often do this instinctively; they'll often tie a woollen sock or stocking around the throat to keep the warmth in – the astral body will start to be attracted to the warmth. It is not attracted to other things such as water or air, but it is attracted to warmth. So if you have had the child in bed for a time like this and the astral body has been drawn there all the time, it will again and again have been attracted to this part here [drawing on the board]. You should then take a piece of cloth and put a bit of warm water on it that contains a few drops of lemon juice and put the cloth around the part. This will draw the irritated part together, so that it will again be open to the astral body, and you can cure the whooping cough very nicely. You just have to do it all the right way, one thing after the other.

Effective treatment depends on one's ability to see through the whole human being and on doing things properly and in the right order. You must also take care in following this procedure that the child does not take fright. For when the child takes fright, the astral body will always come out a little, and this will undo the whole thing.

If we truly cure the child, the whooping cough will run its course and he'll not have asthma later on. If we do it wrongly, the 'fissures' in the wind pipe or tubes will heal up, and the child will seem to have recovered, but the astral body will not have gone in completely, always remaining a little bit outside. Now if a person is very weak, if the child is a weakling, he'll get asthma right away, because the breathing-out process is never quite right. The astral body is not completely involved. An astral body that is outside cannot be properly involved in the breathing-out process. But if the child is a bit stronger, he'll use the other part of the astral body, with the result that the rest of the astral body will only show its weakness at a later time in life, when another illness comes, for instance if the child later gets influenza or something of that kind. And he'll then develop asthma.

You can penetrate the human being very well in this way. You'll find out when the soul principle gets involved and when it does not.

But just look at someone with asthma. The astral body is active. It is scratching away inside all the time, just as the frog scratched its side when you put acid on it. So there you have it, gentlemen, there you have the astral body behaving like a frog, like a turtle. We can actually study the way our astral body behaves by looking at the lower animals. Things would go very differently if the head could be involved in this activity of the astral body. It is something we cannot get at with the head. That is the situation. We are not yet human in the astral body. We are human in our physical bodies on earth, but we are not human in our astral bodies here on earth.

What is the result of this? The result is that this astral body also behaves like an incomplete being. It behaves in an animal way. Imagine therefore you are bringing someone up by beating him all the time. It is really strange how common this method of education by beating still is. There is someone today—he does not interest me in other respects, I find him boring—but here he is most interesting. He has been all over Europe, he's also been in Basel— Rabindranath Tagore,[30] a gentleman who is casting his spell on people today. You know how it is—someone from Asia, that's something new and different, that's what draws the crowds. A European might do so much more, but an Asian, that interests them—a rare animal! You see, he has now written his biography. This biography is really quite boring as well; but it is really important to read the first chapters of this biography. There he writes of how he was always beaten by everyone. Someone who is now one of the scholarly Asians, scholarly Indians, travelling all over Europe, tells that the whole of education really consisted in beating the children all the time. So it is not just a European characteristic. We see from this biography that people in Asia have also been beaten a terrible lot.

Now, as you know, Tagore then became a writer, became all kinds of things, and so it does not show so much any more. But when someone is beaten all the time as a child this will not only have an effect on the physical body but also on the astral body, especially because in children the head is not involved all the time. And the result is that the astral body is then like a cringing dog that has been beaten all the time. You can clearly tell a dog that's been beaten from one that has been raised in a loving way. And it's the same for people. When they are beaten as children—later life may give them a bit more courage, but the astral body continues to cringe for the whole of life, because it is still at the animal level.

So you see, gentlemen, here you can see that it is not just physical beatings that go into the astral body. They will at most cause weals. We carry the moral impressions gained in life on earth in our astral bodies. And it is indeed so that someone who has been beaten a lot in his childhood will later have an astral body that is like a cringing dog. Someone else has hit his teachers—you also get people like that—and his astral body is like a lion. One looks like that inwardly—we might also say in our souls, or let's say astrally, because 'soul' has become quite an abstract word already, with people no longer thinking anything of it—

inwardly, astrally, one assumes a different form of one kind or another, depending on the moral impressions gained in life.

But that is how it is for the whole of life. A slavish person will take things differently from someone who is free and independent. The slave will accept anything. His astral body then bends down and does have something of a cringing dog. An independent character will not accept anything. His astral body then becomes a little bit more human. Here we get some insight into what happens with human beings during their life on earth.

But, gentlemen, we also die. We have been considering this. Only the physical body drops away, goes away. But the figure I have just described remains. You take this through death with you. And someone who has gained higher knowledge by the means I have described, especially in my book *Knowledge of the Higher Worlds*, can clearly see the character a person takes through death. The moral impression of life is in there. You then have to go into the world out of which you create your next life on earth.

Now, gentlemen, if you went into the world out of which you create your next life on earth with an astral body that has come to be as it is because of beatings received in life, you might perhaps become a dog. But a human being cannot become a dog; that is the situation. A human being comes through death out of the moral impressions gained in life in such a way that he might become something or other that comes from the moral impression gained. Someone who has shown courage might become a lion. Maybe some people would be pleased to be a lion in a future life. But a human being cannot actually be a lion because he is not made that way by the world, the cosmos. Someone else may feel a bit like a cat; he'd like to be a cat.

You know, people who lack understanding will raise the objection that anthroposophists say the soul goes into animals later on. The transmigration of souls is said to make the soul go into the animals later on. This is nonsense, of course. What is true is that the soul keeps an impression — you are lion-like, cat-like, tiger-like, crocodile-like when you have died. And because one has to be a human being again, this has to be put aside. This is done during that one-third-the-length-of-life period of which I have spoken before. Someone who lived to the age of 60 will need 20 years for this. This is not mere invention. We know it to be such, for oddly enough the human being becomes like that when he enters into sleep at night. This is merely in preparation. And sleep takes up altogether a third of life. Such a third of life, a period, therefore, that takes up a third of one's lifetime, is needed to free oneself from the moral impression.

But, gentlemen, you don't know anything about the whole business you go through between going to sleep and waking up. And that is a good thing. For it means the moral impression gained only comes through a little bit as our conscience. When one is obliged to look at it all, it comes through much more strongly.

And why is it that only a little bit of what we have experienced in sleep comes through, as conscience, after we wake up? It is because we go down into the physical body. This covers it up. Otherwise one would remember when one wakes up in the morning what sleep has been telling one, and what a dreadful fellow one really is. For one has learned this during sleep. It sometimes haunts us a little in our sleep. And dreams which are a bit haunted by knowing what a dreadful fellow one really is are particularly interesting to study. Generally, however, we know nothing about it. But when we do not have a physical body after death, everything we have in the astral body comes into the I, and so we then have it in the I. We then have to go through the whole period. When we have laid the astral body aside, the things we have laid aside are then only in the I. But we are then able to prepare cleanly for the right physical body in our next life. This takes as long as I have told you before.

So you see, we only need to take a good look at the human being as he is now in his life on earth to get absolutely the right idea of how these four principles in man—physical body, ether body, astral body, I—are related.

You see, gentlemen, let me tell you something else. Imagine this is the human heart [Fig. 22]. So there it sits. Two nerve strands go to the heart. They come from back there, go down there and then to the heart. There goes one, which then spreads out in the heart. And then there is another, and this also spreads out in the heart. Imagine I now let an electric current pass through the nerve. I'll then see something strange. The heart will start to beat faster and faster. Why? The electric current stimulates the nerve and this makes the heart beat faster and faster. The electric current stimulates the nerve.

But now imagine I do not galvanize this nerve but the other one, the second one. Now you might think a nerve is a

Fig. 22

nerve. I apply the electric current. And you would think, wouldn't you, that the heart will start to beat faster and faster again. But that is not the way it is. When I galvanize this nerve here [the first one], the heart beats faster and faster. When I galvanize this one [the second one], the heart beats more and more slowly. And if I put a really strong current through it, the heart will stop beating altogether. I have to stop immediately, or the individual will die of heart failure. Now the fact is that there is absolutely no difference between these two nerves as far as their construction goes. They are both made the same way. What, then, is happening here?

You see, it is like this. When this part here is galvanized the astral body goes in there, stimulates the heart, so that it beats faster because something it normally has to do itself has been taken over by the electric current. It can therefore work faster in the heart. But let us assume the current is applied here [the other nerve]. Now the astral body wants to make the heart move faster, but an obstacle is put in its way from the other side. As soon as it wants to make the heart move faster, it cannot get through on the other side. This stimulus [first nerve] helps the heart by taking over some of the work. This stimulation [second nerve] hinders it because it comes from the opposite direction. If I were able to get inside the heart and apply the electric stimulus from there, this, too, would make the heart beat faster. But when I galvanize this nerve from outside, the astral body cannot move the heart because it meets more and more of an obstacle.

You see from this that it is possible to know exactly how this really happens in the human body, with the astral body on its part taking action just as I would if I wanted to turn a wheel. There I push, and I continue turning the wheel; but when I want to turn it the other way, it won't do it. That is how it is with the heart, that is how it is with the lung, with every organ. Every organ is supplied with nerves from two sides; but it is the astral body which is actually taking action.

Now you might say: 'Well, perhaps it is the head after all which is active in the case of the astral body?' No, gentlemen, if it were the head you would have to apply your electric current up at the head. But that would not get you anywhere; you have to galvanize from that point. If you cut off the head as far as the astral body is concerned, it will still find the spot, just as with the frog, or the turtle. You have to galvanize where the nerve is, for even the frog still has it. This spot is called the medulla oblongata, a continuation of the spinal marrow. This is where you have to apply the electric current, and the head need not be involved at all.

Other things also show quite clearly that the head need not be involved. First of all, just think, if you would have to let the beating of the heart be done from the head, that would be a pretty kettle of fish! The heart needs to beat 72 times a minute, and you would therefore have to think of your heart 72 times a minute. And your heart would have to stop whilst you were asleep. The head thus cannot help when it comes to these movements which take place inside the human being. They are done the way it is done in a frog or a turtle.

If we have asthma, these internal movements are done in an abnormal way; in health they are done in a healthy way. You see from this that everything that happens by way of movements and so on inside the human being happens unconsciously, governed by the astral body.

And it is this astral body which after death must first hand over to the I, as it were, the moral impression it has gained of the world. The I will then be able to create a further human life on earth. Because of this the years after death, when we live in such a way that we are able to lay aside the inner astral configuration we have gained in life, are such that we can prepare again for a new life on earth in which we can be truly human.

And how do we bring the fruits of our previous life into the new human life? Well you see, gentlemen, it is like this. The child sleeps in the early part of his life. If he had conscious awareness, he would not be able to bring the things the I has brought with it to realization. They have merely been learned from the astral body. The I is still in the astral body; only it does not need to be involved in the work before conception. It is the astral body which has to work, the astral world has to work from the stars, the way I showed you the other day. The child must come into life asleep; he learns to walk, learns to talk, learns to think. Into his walking, talking and thinking he pours the moral impulse from the previous life and selects. That is our destiny.

It does not limit our freedom. I think I have told you this before. We have our destiny in us; we prepare our own destiny. But this does not limit our freedom, just as it is not limited by the fact that we have black or blond hair, brown or blue eyes, or are unable to reach out and touch the moon. Our freedom is not limited by the fact that we bring things with us from our previous life so that we may be one thing or another as human beings. People differ because they bring different things with them from their previous life on earth.

Now you might well say: 'This takes us back to a point where we think that we return for ever and ever to live new lives on earth.' No, gentlemen, there was a time on earth when human beings got no further than infants do today. With the earth still thick, not surrounded by air but by a thick sauce — you'll remember the things I have told you about the earth — human beings did not need to learn to walk. The thick sauce would support them. Today they have become human in their physical bodies. In their astral bodies they are still at the animal level at which they have been in the past. There they have not brought anything with them, and it has all come about gradually. When human beings learned to walk, talk and think, their destinies also began to evolve. And if human beings are now again learning to take in things of the spirit in their lifetime, they will also get out of the animal habit again and get used to a world in which they will no longer live in a way that involved walking, talking and thinking, but in yet another way.

So there is a space between these two states. And in this in-between space we come back again and again in a particular life.

And now, gentlemen, there is one more question. We'll have to consider this the next time, at 9 o'clock next Wednesday. It is this important question which comes up again and again, where someone says: 'It's all right for you to talk about the previous life on earth. But I don't remember it. I won't believe anything that I cannot remember.' I'll explain to you about this remembering the next time we meet, what it is about. This will have taken us a bit further again, and we shall more or less have covered the question for which we have been preparing.

Why do we not remember earlier lives on earth?

Good morning, gentlemen! Let us now add some more on the matter we have been considering. As I said at the end of our last meeting, the main objection people raise is that the things they hear about life before we enter into an earthly body and also about earlier lives may indeed be true—but why do they not remember any of it? The first thing I'll do today, therefore, will be to show you in detail why we don't remember and what memory is about.

To start with we have to give some thought to the human body, for it really is indeed important to put these things in a scientific way.

You see, in this respect, when it comes to the question of repeated earth lives, people are really quite funny in the way they judge others who did or do know something about these repeated earth lives. A great figure in German literature was Lessing, who lived in the eighteenth century.[31] Lessing's achievements were tremendous, and he is still generally acknowledged to this day. Professors speaking about Lessing at German universities will often stay on the subject for months. As you know, a book by a Lessing expert has actually appeared in social-democratic literature, a big book on Lessing by Franz Mehring.[32] He presents Lessing from a different point of view. We can't say that what he says is right; but at any rate, social-democratic literature now includes a big book on Lessing. In short, Lessing is considered a very great man. As a very old man Lessing, whose plays are still performed at many theatres and much appreciated, wrote a relatively short work called 'Educating, or bringing up, the human race'. At

the end of the book we read that we really won't get anywhere in considering the human soul, that we really cannot
have proper knowledge of the inner life, unless we assume
there to be repeated lives on earth, and if we reflect on this,
we really come to see things the way primitive peoples did
in the past. For they did all believe in repeated earth lives.
Humanity only gave this up later, when people became
'modern'. And Lessing said that he could see no reason why
something should be nonsense just because people believed
it in earliest times. In short, he himself said he could only
manage with the inner life of man if he held to this original
belief in repeated earth lives.

Now as you can imagine, this is highly embarrassing for
present-day 'scientists', as they are called. They will say:
'Lessing was one of the greatest people of all times. But
those repeated earth lives were nonsense. What is one to do
with this? Well, Lessing was old then. He'd grown feeble-
minded. We don't accept the repeated earth lives.' You see,
that is the way these people are. They will accept the things
that suit them and call the person concerned a great man.
But if he ever said anything that does not suit them, then
they say he was feeble-minded at the time.

Very odd things will sometimes happen. There was the
great scientist Sir William Crookes, for example.[33] Well, I
don't agree with everything he says, but he is certainly
considered to be one of the great scientists. He lived in our
time, at the end of the nineteenth century. He'd always do
scientific work in the mornings. He'd go to his laboratory,
and he made great discoveries. We would not have some of
these things—X-rays and so on—if Crookes had not done
the preliminary work. In the afternoons, however, he would
always study psychology. As I said, I do not agree with
everything, but that is what he did. And surely people thus
also had to say: 'Well then, he must have been intelligent in
the mornings and stupid in the afternoons—bright and

stupid at the same time!' That's the way things are in the world.

Now there's something else. You will always hear—I spoke about this when I was talking about the colours—that scientists consider Newton to be the greatest scientist of all times. He wasn't, but they think so. And again we have an embarrassment. This man Newton, considered the greatest scientist, also wrote a book on the Book of Revelation,[34] which is usually found at the end of the Bible. Another embarrassment, therefore.

In short, people who altogether deny that it is possible to study the psyche, the soul, are profoundly embarrassed by the greatest scientists of all people, and also the greatest historians. The point is that anyone who takes science really seriously cannot help himself but to extend his search for knowledge also to the soul. And the opportunities for this are always given. As I told you, one simply needs to observe. Now it is not possible to see everything directly by looking at everyday life, especially if one has not studied it beforehand. Nature, and sometimes humanity, also does experiments for us, experiments we need not design artificially. Once they have been done, however, we can study them. We can take our guidance from them, or at least pick up ideas. There is one experiment that is really important, characteristic, if we want to have something valid concerning the inner life of man. Everyone accepts the physical body, otherwise they would have to deny existence to the human being altogether. It is not in dispute. Everyone has it. In modern science the view is that the physical body is the only one, and everything has to be explained in terms of the physical body.

There is something, however, which will immediately show us that the human being also has the other three bodies—the invisible ether body, the astral body and the I— if we observe it properly. One thing can be observed in a completely scientific way—there are many things, but one in particular can be observed in a completely scientific way. It shows that human beings may indeed get into states where they show us that the ether body exists, and the astral body, and the I.

You see some people in Europe feel the need to numb their minds. Many other means are used today. I have told you that people use cocaine, for instance, to numb their minds.[35] But opium has been used in Europe at all times. There have always been people who have been dissatisfied with life, or had too many problems, not knowing what to do, and they would drug themselves with opium. They would always take just a small amount of opium. What happened then? To begin with, if someone takes a small amount of opium he gets into a state where he experiences things inwardly; he is no longer thinking, but begins to dream, seeing wild, chaotic images. He likes it, it puts him at his ease. The dreams get more and more intoxicating. Some will then enter into blank despair, bethink themselves and begin to behave like sinners; others start to rant and rage, even feeling murderous. And then they go to sleep. Taking opium thus means that people take a poison into their bodies so that they enter vehemently into a state which then gradually merges into sleep.

If we consider what is really happening here in the human being we find—one can see it—that they first of all get into very excited dreams, starting to fantasize, and then go to sleep. So something has gone away from them. The element has gone away from them that makes them sensible people, something that lives in them to make them sensible. That has gone. But before it goes, and even after it has gone, they live in the wildest, most chaotic and excited dreams. After a time they'll wake up again and be restored to normal, up to a point, until they take opium again. They thus make themselves into sleeping people, but vehemently so.

We can see that when someone goes to sleep under the influence of opium the principle that is active in him is not the one that makes him sensible but the one that gives him life; otherwise he would not wake up again, he would have to die. The principle is active in him that gives him life for the moment. And we can see that during the night, too, something of a struggle takes place in the body so that we may wake up again. Something is active in the human being that does not include the sensible part; it is the element that gives life to the body. The poison makes the person's body die a little. This drives away common sense. But the life-giving element is still in him, for otherwise he would not wake up again. What has therefore been influenced by the opium? The principle that gives life. Taking small amounts of opium has influenced the ether body.

But now imagine someone takes too much or deliberately poisons himself with opium. The effect is not the same then. It is a strange thing, but now only the thing which happens last when a little opium is taken will happen. What happens last in that case will come first if a lot of opium is taken. The individual will immediately go to sleep. The principle that gives one sense will not go away slowly then, but quickly, very quickly. Something remains in the person, however, that was not in him at all when he took just a little opium. Again this is something we can see.

So let us assume someone takes so much opium that he is really poisoned. The first thing that happens will be that he goes to sleep. But then the body will begin to get restless, unreasonable; he is breathing stertorously, snoring; then he'll have fits. And you'll notice something very peculiar, for his face will be quite red and his lips quite blue.

Now remember what I told you last time. I said that breathing problems always come when we breathe out. Now what is snoring, for instance—first stertorous breathing, then snoring—what is it really? You see people who cannot breathe out properly will snore. When we breathe out properly — if that is the mouth [Fig. 23], then the air goes in, and after some time it goes out again. And in the air passage is the uvula. You can see it if you look in the mouth. And up there is something that goes up and down, the velum, the soft palate. This moves. The uvula and the soft palate are moving all the time as we breathe in and out, if it goes normally. But if you breathe in and then do not breathe out properly, so that it eructs, then this part, the soft palate and the uvula, starts to tremble and this produces the stertorous breathing and then snoring.

Fig. 23

You can see from this that it has something to do with our breathing. Someone who just drugs himself with a little opium gets into those other states I have described to you — a kind of delirium, a rage. He will slowly go to sleep. But if he goes to sleep quickly, having taken a large amount of opium, he starts snoring and gets fits; his face turns red, his lips blue. For as I told you, human beings have red blood because they breathe in oxygen. When the blood mixes with oxygen it turns red; when it mixes with carbon it turns blue. When it is breathed out, it is blue. So if you see someone with a red face and blue lips, what does it mean? Yes, there is too much breathed-in air beneath the face, too much red blood because of breathing in. And what does it mean when the lips are blue? Then there is too much of the blood that should really go out. It piles up in there. It could indeed go on to the place in the lung where the carbon dioxide then comes free, where carbon dioxide can be breathed out. So when someone is poisoned by opium the situation is that the whole of his breathing is held up. And because of that you get the red blood in the face on the one hand and the blue blood in the lips on the other.

This is tremendously interesting, gentlemen. What are the lips? You see, the lips are highly peculiar organs in the face. To have a face you really need to draw it like this [Fig. 24], with skin on the outside everywhere. It is covered with skin on the outside everywhere. But on the lips it is really a piece of inner skin. There the inner becomes outer. It is a piece of inner skin. The human being opens up his inner nature to the outside by having lips. If the lips are blue, therefore, rather than red, it means that everything inside has too much blue blood in it. So you see that when someone has opium poisoning the body sends all unused blood to the surface, and sends all blue blood to the inside.

Fig. 24

This is something else primitive peoples once knew, this business of the blue blood going inside. When someone had too much blue blood inside they would say that someone who has too much blue blood inside him is in the first place someone who has little soul; his soul has gone away. 'Blue-blooded' therefore became a term of abuse. And when members of the nobility were called blue-blooded, people wanted to say their souls were not there. It is strange how these things live in a most marvellous way in popular wisdom. You really can learn a tremendous amount from language.

You can now see that this is something that has an effect in the human being but not, for instance, in a plant. For if you introduce a poison into a plant, the poison stays up above in some way; it does not spread. Belladonna, deadly nightshade, is a very poisonous plant. It keeps its poison up above and does not let it go into the whole plant. When a human being takes such a poison the effect is that it involves the whole body, driving the red blood to the outside and the blue blood inside. Yes, plants also have life. Those plants have their ether body in them, they have the principle in them which in people is left blue with small amounts of opium taken, not with large amounts. That will make the human being sentient. If a plant had blood it would also be sentient, as human beings are and animals. Humans and animals have this without taking opium when the ether body is in conflict with the physical body; the blood is then immediately pushed to the outside, and something remains behind in the body, and this puts things out of order in the body. This is the astral body. We are thus able to say that the astral body is influenced when much opium is taken.

The third way of taking opium is widespread in the world, though not in Europe—more among certain Turks, for instance, and above all in Asia and Indochina, among the Malays. These people always only take as much opium as they are just able to tolerate and therefore wake up again properly and do not die of it. They therefore go through everything opium eaters go through, which is most interesting. Only they gradually get habituated, and then they go through the process more consciously. The Turks thus say: 'Yes, I was in Paradise when I had taken opium.' So that is indeed how it is when the fantastic developments come. And the Malays in Indochina would also like to see all this. They therefore get the opium habit because they would like to see it all. This is something people can do for a relatively long time and we therefore have to say to ourselves that there must clearly also be something else.

Now one would have to say that if these people who eat opium from habit — it is a real habit with them — if these dreamers were to see only this they would surely get tired of it after a time. But, you see, it is a most peculiar thing. These people are descended from the first people on earth, people who still knew something of the eternal soul, the soul that goes through different lives on earth. They knew something of this. It is something people have lost today. And these people who have not gone through European civilization use opium to put themselves in a position where they can feel something of the soul's eternal life. It is indeed a terrible thing, but they will again and again induce a disease in themselves. At the present time a healthy body cannot know anything of the soul's immortality unless a person makes special mental efforts. And because of this these people are gradually ruining their bodies, so that the soul principle is gradually forced out.

You can see something very peculiar when you look at people who take opium habitually and therefore also survive for a time. They grow very pale after a time. They may have had a good skin colour earlier on, but now they will be pale.

It means something different among Malays than it would among Europeans, for they are yellowy brown and therefore really look like spectres when they grow pale. Then, after some time, they look as if their faces were quite hollow around the eyes. They then begin to grow skinny, and even before that will no longer be able to walk properly. They merely hobble along. Then they also no longer want to think and grow extremely forgetful. In the end they have a stroke.

[writing on the board]

Physical body	
Ether body	taking small amounts of opium
Astral body	taking large amounts of opium
I	habitual use of opium

Those are the phenomena. It is very interesting to observe it. Before their limbs grow clumsy they get severe constipation, which means their intestines are no longer functioning. You can see from the things I have told you that the whole body is gradually undermined.

Now there is something highly peculiar here. Not much is known yet about this because people do not pay attention to it; but it is something one can see quite easily. It is well known how these people become opium eaters; that has been described often enough. But now just let them try — after all they try things out often enough in other respects today — and give the dose a habitual opium eater takes to an animal. The animal will either get a little bit lively, which would be the first stage, where the ether body is thrown into chaos, or it will get to the second stage, if given enough, and die. You do not get the condition I have just described, the condition of the habitual opium eater, in animals. You do not get this in animals.

What does this tell us, gentlemen? Well, it shows that when opium in that strength gets into the astral body, causing the relationship between blue and red blood to change, the situation is that in animals blue and red blood are all the time shooting one into the other in a horizontal direction. In a human being, who learns to walk upright, blue and red blood does not exactly shoot in that direction [drawing on the board], but from top to bottom and from below upwards. It is because of this that human beings can be habitual opium eaters.

Now I have been telling you that human beings have an I because they are upright. Animals do not have an I, for their backs are horizontal. So what is affected by habitual opium eating? — the I. We are thus able to say: I — habitual opium consumption. And by considering opium we have now discovered all the three supersensible human bodies — the ether body with opium taken in small amounts, the astral body with opium taken in large amounts, and the I with opium taken habitually. So you see how one can develop this most beautifully in a scientific way; one must only be able to observe properly.

You'll now also see that a Malay who is a habitual opium eater comes to something tremendous. He comes to the I. And what does he get? What is this Malay or this Turk looking forward to as he follows his opium habit? He looks forward to it because his memory comes awake in a most wonderful way. He will quickly get a view of his whole earth life and much more. On the one hand it is terrible, for he is making his body sick by doing this. But on the other hand the desire to get to know the I has such a powerful effect in him that he just cannot resist. He is simply delighted when this gigantic memory is produced.

But, you see, it is like this. When someone does something to excess it will ruin him. If he works too much it will ruin him; if he thinks too much it will ruin him. And when someone is all the time calling up a tremendous power of memory, this will ruin his body. All the things I have described to you simply come from a memory that is too powerful. That is what comes first. And later—I have described it to you—the person grows slack in his walking. He no longer remembers inwardly how he should put his feet forward. This is unconscious memory. Then he grows forgetful. And it is exactly in achieving his aim that he is ruined. But it is possible to see, to be aware, that the I is present when opium has become a habit.

What happens in modern science? Well, if you open a book you will find the things I have told you. You find it said that people grow delirious with small doses of opium, and so on, and if they take large doses they will first go to sleep and their bodies will immediately be destroyed. They die, their faces having turned red and their lips blue. And all these things also come with habitual opium eating. But all this refers only to the physical body and what happens in it. You can read that opium eaters develop stertorous breathing, get fits, snore. You can read that they lose weight, are no longer able to walk, grow forgetful and finally have a stroke, because their memory is destroying the brain—for that is how we should see it. Everything is described, but it is all related to the physical body.

And that is nonsense, of course. Otherwise everything physical could only be said to relate to the physical body. All the phenomena that appear there can also be seen in plants. Yet we cannot say that man is just a plant. For with opium taken in high doses the effect shows itself in the astral body, and the phenomena relating to habitual opium use are only seen in human beings. If animals had something to gain from opium use and did not die of it immediately you would see many animals simply eating the opium found in plants. Why would they do so? Because animals eat the things they eat from habit. So if opium eating would benefit them, they would eat the opium in plants. If they do not do so, this is simply because they would not gain anything by it.

All this can be discovered by means of science. But we now have to consider if all this — the memory a Malay gains by making himself sick — can also be gained in a healthy way. Here we must remember that the earliest people knew that human beings live on earth again and again. Lessing said, as I told you, that he could see no reason why something should be nonsense just because people believed it in earliest times. Those early people simply did not have the kind of abstract thinking we have today. They did not have science either. They saw everything in mythological terms. Looking at a plant they would not study it and say that there were particular forces in it; they would say that it had particular spiritual elements in it. They saw everything in images and they were altogether still living more in the spirit ... [gap in text]. The situation is that human beings were then able to develop in such a way through progress that they came to live more in the physical body. This alone made it possible for them to be free, otherwise they would always have been influenced. The people of earliest times were not free; but they did still see things in the spirit. The way we are now, gentlemen, we do truly have the abstract ideas in which we are drilled even at school. You see, we are actually able to say that the most important activities of which humanity is so proud today are really something abstract.

Speaking to the teachers who are here in Dornach I said yesterday that when a child gets to be about seven years old he is supposed to learn something. He should learn, having learned his whole life up to now, that the individual he sees before him is his father and that this [writing *f a t h e r* on the board] means 'father'. He is suddenly supposed to learn this. But it has no connection with his father. Those are strange signs that have nothing at all to do with his father!

The child is supposed to learn it all of a sudden. He'll resist, for his father is a man who has that kind of hair, such a nose; that is what the child has always seen. He'll resist the notion that those signs are meant to be his father.

The child has learned to exclaim 'ah!' when he was amazed. Now he is suddenly expected to think that *this* [pointing to the letter] is an 'a'. The whole thing is completely abstract and does not relate to anything the child has learned until now. So we must first build a bridge, so that the child is able to learn such a thing. Let me show you how such a bridge may be built.

You may, for example, say to the child: 'Look. What's that?' [Fig. 25, left]. If you draw this for the child and ask him what it is, what will he say? He'll say: 'A fish! That's a fish.' He'll not say, 'I can't tell what it is.' There [the written-down *father*] he can't say: 'I can tell it's my father.' But he will recognize the fish.

Fig. 25

I then say: 'Say the word fish; then leave out the "i" and what comes after it, and say just "F". Look, let me draw it for you: *F*.' I have thus taken the F from the fish. The child will first draw a fish and then come to the letter F. You just have to do it in a sensible way so that it'll not be abstract but come out of the image. And then the child will of course be happy to learn. It is something we can do with every letter. You just have to gradually get into the way of it.

One of the teachers at our Waldorf school once showed most beautifully how Roman figures came into existence. When he got to the V, it suddenly would not work. How can one get the V? Well, just look — what is this? [He held up his hand.] Of course you'll say that a hand is always a hand. But surely we can see something in it? *I, II, III, IIII, V* fingers. Let me draw this hand on the board [Fig. 25, third form] in this way, with two things extended [the thumb and then the other four fingers]. Now I have a hand with the V [five] in it; it is definitely a five. I now draw it in a slightly simpler form and you have got the Roman figure V from a hand that has five fingers.

So you see, gentlemen, the situation is that we are suddenly thrown into a completely abstract world nowadays. We learn to write, we learn to read, and it has nothing to do with life. And that is how we have lost the things which people had who were not yet able to write and read.

Now you should not do as our opponents do and say: 'That man Steiner told us in class that people were more intelligent when they did not yet have writing and reading.' And they'll immediately go on to say: 'He does not want people to learn to write and read any more.' That is not my intention. People should always keep pace with their civilization, and certainly learn to write and to read. But we also should not lose the things that can indeed be lost through writing and reading. We need to take the spiritual view to discover what human life is like.

Let me now tell you something quite simple about two people. One of them takes off his shirt collar when he undresses at night — it has two little studs, one at the back and one in front, and I am taking this example because I am wearing such a collar. One of the two people does it without giving it any thought, undoing one stud and then the other and getting into bed. In the morning he'll run around and look everywhere in the room, asking: 'Where are my collar studs?' He cannot find them. He does not remember where he put them. Why? Because he did not give them any thought.

Now the other person. He has not exactly developed the habit of always putting his collar stud in the same place—which would be the lazy way—but he says to himself: 'When I put the little studs down, I put the one next to the candlestick and the other one over there.' He thus gives the matter some thought and does not merely put them down in a thoughtless way. Now when he gets up in the morning he'll go straight there, pick up the studs from where he put them, and have no need to hunt for them all over the room: 'Where are my collar studs? Where have I put my collar studs?' So what is the difference? The difference is that one man has given a matter some thought and then remembered, and that the other man did not give it any thought and does not remember. Now you can only remember things in the morning—it is no good to go to bed at night and then try and remember—you will only remember things in the morning when you have given them some thought the night before.

Gentlemen, let us take a bit of a look at history now. According to what I told you before, all our souls have been here at a time when only few people had as yet learned to think. People did not think at all in earlier times. In earliest times they lived in the spirit. And it was abnormal for someone to think in those times. During the Middle Ages people did not yet think at all. They have only started to think from the fifteenth century onwards; they did not take everything into their thoughts the way we do. This can be proved by historians. No wonder then that you don't remember your earlier lives! Now people have learned to think. We are at a time in historical evolution when people have learned to think. And in their next life they will remember this present life just as someone remembers his collar studs in the morning.

It means that if someone now learns to think of the things in the world in the right way, learns to think the way I have shown you, it will be just as it is when he thinks of his collar stud. The modern way in science is a way where people do not think of their collar studs. If someone just gives a description: 'Delirium develops, the lips turn blue and the face red,' and so on, the situation is that in his next life he will not think of the things that are most important. He'll not remember at all, throwing everything into confusion, like the person who creates confusion in his room because he has to go out and he cannot find his things. Someone who thinks, however, that it simply comes from ether body, astral body, I, will learn to think in such a way that he will be able to remember properly in his next life on earth. It will only show itself then. And today only few people are instructed on how to do things because only few individuals have known about it in their last life on earth. They now find out about it and are able to tell others about it. And if they do the things I have written in my books, if they do what it says in *Knowledge of the Higher Worlds*, it may happen that they realize even in this life that they have lived earlier lives on earth. But we are only just beginning with the anthroposophical science of the spirit. And people will gradually be able to remember again.

Now people will say: 'Yes, but one can't remember it; and if someone does not remember earlier lives on earth this means he cannot have had those earlier lives on earth.' We might just as well also say: 'A human being is unable to do sums; we can prove that a human being cannot do sums. He is a human being but he cannot do sums.' And to prove it someone brings in a four-year-old child and shows that the child cannot do sums. This is a human being, but he cannot do sums! We'll tell him: 'He'll learn, never fear. Knowing human nature we know that he'll learn to do sums.' And if someone refers to someone today who cannot remember his earlier lives on earth we have to tell him: 'Yes, but nothing was done in the past to help people remember. Quite the contrary, there are still many people today who have not caught up with the times, and they want to keep others in ignorance, so that they will know nothing of the spirit, have no idea as to what they should remember in their next life on earth, and get quite confused, like the man with his collar stud.' People must first of all learn to think in life about the things they should remember later on.

Anthroposophy exists to draw people's attention to the things they should later remember. And people who want to prevent anthroposophy actually want to keep people in ignorance, so that they will not remember. And it is important, gentlemen, for us to realize that human beings must first of all learn to use their thoughts in the right way. Today they want to define thoughts and demand that books should give the right definitions. That is something people knew even in ancient Greece, gentlemen. There was someone then who specially wanted to train people in making definitions. Today they tell you in school: 'You have to learn: What is light?' I knew a boy at school once; we were in primary school together, then I went to another school and he trained to be a teacher at a teachers' training college. I met him again at the age of 17. By then he had become a real teacher. So I asked him: 'What did you learn about light?' He said: 'Light is the cause of the ability to see bodies.' Nothing wrong with that. We might just as well say: 'What is poverty?' 'Poverty comes from having no money!' It is more or less the same kind of definition. But people have to learn a great deal of such stuff.

Now there was someone in ancient Greece who made fun

of that kind of clever learning even then. Children have learned at school: 'What is a human being?' 'A human being is a living creature with two legs and no feathers.' A boy who was a particularly sharp thinker took a cockerel, plucked it, and brought the plucked cockerel to show his teacher the next day, saying: 'Sir, is that a human being? It has no feathers and has two legs!' That was the power of definition. And the things we generally still find in our books are more or less in line with such definitions.

All books, including social books people write, refer to the condition of life more or less the way a definition is made: 'A human being is a living creature with two legs and no feathers.' Further conclusions are then drawn. Of course, if you have a book with a definition to start with, you can draw all kinds of logical conclusions; but it will never fit the human being; it may also be true for a cockerel that has been plucked. That is the way our definitions are! What matters is that we must see the thing the way it really is.

The truth of the matter is that we have to say [referring back to the table of the human bodies in relation to opium use]: physical body; ether body, affected by opium taken in small amounts; astral body, affected by large amounts; the I affected by opium taken as a habit. And working with the science of the spirit, getting to know the human being in a way one does not merely describe things as if in a dream: 'Such and such conditions occur,' but really knows: 'That is where the astral body is active; there the ether body is active; in there the I is active,' one has real thoughts and not just definitions. And if we have taken in real thoughts in our present life on earth and not just definitions, we will remember the present life on earth in the right way. Now it is only possible to remember earlier lives on earth with great effort, as I have described it. Later we shall remember it well, if we do not make ourselves ill, for instance by taking opium, if we do not influence the body, but do exercises in mind and spirit that will make it possible for the soul truly to know the spirit.

So you see that a science of the spirit is in fact developing in anthroposophy. You can be sure that in anthroposophy we are not wanting to be superstitious. You get people who hear something unusual reported about spiritualistic things and they'll then say: 'Surely it is as if a world of the spirit is revealed in this.' But the world of the spirit reveals itself in the human being! If people sit around a table and get it to knock they'll say: 'There must be a spirit in there.' But when four people are sitting there, you have four spirits! You only have to get to know them. But people prefer to do things unconsciously. A medium has to be there. Just look at the newspaper cutting you gave me a few weeks ago, for example.[36] There you read that somewhere in England people got tremendously excited because things fell off shelves during the night, windows got broken, and so on. What struck me most about this—one must of course have seen it for oneself before one can really talk about it—but what struck me most was that the report also stated that those people had a whole horde of cats. Well, if you have a horde of cats and two or three of them run riot, you can indeed see these 'spiritual phenomena' happening. But, as I said, one would have to know the story properly; only then can one really speak about it.

You see, people once urged me strongly to attend a spiritualist seance. Well, I said I'd do so, for you can really only judge such matters if you've seen them. Now the medium was very famous, and when everyone had sat down, and had first had their minds numbed a bit by some music—everyone sat there numb in mind—the medium started to have flowers come down out of the air all the time, just the kind of thing one would expect. Every medium has an 'impresario', a manager, which is part of being a proper medium. Well, the people paid their obolus, a financial contribution, having had their enjoyment. For the organizers this was of course the important thing, that a contribution was paid. And I said — people are terribly fanatical about these things, they'll start a fight with you if you want to tell them the truth, it is just people like this who are the worst — but there were some who had sense and I said to them they should investigate things on another occasion, not at the end but at the beginning, and they would find the flowers in the manager's humped back. You'll always find that this is how things are.

Superstition has to be left behind, gentlemen, if we want to speak of the world of the spirit. One should never be deceived, not by mad cats nor by a hump-backed manager. We only find the spirit if we no longer fall for superstitions but always do things in a truly scientific way.

Sleeping and waking — life after death — the Christ
spirit — the two Jesus children

Good morning, gentlemen! Have you thought of a question?

Speaker: *You were so kind as to tell us what it is like when the spirit has left the body. Me and my colleagues did find we could understand the last lecture very well. But in the [book] Theosophy it says that when the spirit has left the body the soul still has its cravings. We find this a tough nut to crack.*

Rudolf Steiner: Very good. Now tell me the other question as well.

Speaker: *A pamphlet has come into my hands, by chance; it's by a Dr Hauer.[37] I suppose you have read it and therefore know about it. This man Hauer makes you appear as if the things you are saying are nothing new, as if everything said in anthroposophy has been known for a long time, that it is all known already. And he then goes on to say that the thing he has found most incredible in anthroposophy is the story of the two Jesus children.*

[The speaker went on to say that he had to admit that he, too, could not understand the thing about the two Jesus children himself, with one of them coming from another world. No doubt Dr Steiner had the pamphlet himself.]

Rudolf Steiner: Yes, I have the pamphlet, but I have not yet cut the pages.

The speaker then went on to say that if it were not too much to ask, he'd be pleased if Dr Steiner were to say something about the Jesus family.

Another question: *In the last few days my colleagues have asked me about the Christ. So it would please me if Dr Steiner could say something about the Christ spirit.*

Rudolf Steiner: Is there perhaps another question as well, so that we may consider the whole of it?

I'll first of all deal with the question of the desires. The thing is like this. If you consider the things which human beings experience other than those experienced by stones and plants, you will find that human beings experience their world of thought. Plants do not show that they have a world of thought. Thoughts do live in plants, but it would be nonsense to look for conscious thought in a plant.

Now with science often so superficial today, something rather peculiar has come about. Scholars are of all kinds nowadays, and since some of them are not able to believe completely that all processes are merely physical, mineral by nature and without life, they do assume that there is at least a soul element. Not knowing anything about this soul element they will say, therefore: 'The soul element shows itself in the fact that some creature does something or other.'

There are plants that behave in a very strange way. One of them is called the Venus's fly-trap because of the way it behaves.[38] The surface of the broad leaves in the ground rosette is divided into two halves, with three bristle-like outgrowths on each. If an insect lands on the leaf and touches one of these bristly outgrowths the two halves of the leaf fold up so quickly that the small insect is trapped between them. So that is something which exists.

People who talk superficially of the soul and do not know anything about it will say: 'A plant has a soul just as human beings have a soul.' I always have only one thing to say to such people: 'I know a small device; you put some fat bacon into it, having browned it a little first — a mousetrap. And when a mouse nibbles on the bacon the trap will close of its own accord. Someone who concludes from such things as the Venus's fly-trap that there has to be a soul in there would also have to say that the mousetrap has a soul, for it closes of its own accord.' It always is a matter of how we take the background of anything.

You see, the characteristic of anthroposophy is that we always consider the background. Others who do think there is a soul but know nothing of the soul will say a plant also has a soul if it acts in a similar way to a mousetrap when an insect comes close. In anthroposophy, it is not outer appearances that lead to conclusions but true insight into the soul element. Part of this is that human beings develop cravings. A craving arises, for instance, when one is thirsty. If I'm thirsty I crave a drink of water or something. All right, then, good; the water will quench my thirst. A craving is anything where you wish for, want, something out of the inner organism; that would always be a craving.

Now you see, people never think about one thing. They do not think about the state of soul that exists when someone wakes up. You know, when someone wakes up, these people now investigate how much carbon dioxide is in the blood and so on; that is, they only investigate the physical condition. The truth of the matter is that a human being wakes up because he has a craving for his physical body. When you go to sleep at night you no longer crave your physical body. It is filled to the brim with getting-tired substances. It is no longer a good place to be. The soul — being the I and the astral body — wants to go outside to recover. In the morning, when the physical body has been restored, and the soul which is outside the body has noticed this from the condition of the skin, being close to it — the soul will return to the physical body, for it craves to be in the physical body for as long as the physical body is at all able to live. The soul thus craves to live in the body for the whole of its life.

Now consider something else. You cut your finger and it hurts. This would be the finger [Fig. 26]. You cut it and it hurts. What has actually happened? Well, the physical body

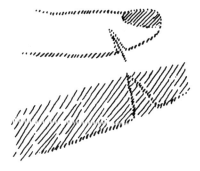

Fig. 26

has been torn apart a little bit. You can cut into the physical body but not into the astral body. Let me now draw in the astral body. If I make it a big cut, you have a gap, and the astral body is in it. It craves to be able to get also into the place where the physical body has been torn apart. It craves to be in the body and cannot do so because the body is torn there. That is the pain.

Now just think, if the soul craves for the physical body throughout life, something has to happen after death.

If you develop a craving for sugar as a child and someone who is important, someone who means something to you, considers it better for you at some stage in your life not to take so much sugar, you will still have your craving for sugar. Let us assume you have developed diabetes and therefore should no longer do it—well, gentlemen, it will take a long time to get out of the habit! You'll always have the craving for sugar and have to get out of the habit gradually. You know, someone who drinks a lot has developed a craving for drink; he'll need to get out of the habit gradually. Someone who eats opium, the way I told you the other day, and people deprive him of it, he'll go quite mad in his craving for opium.

The craving for the body lives in the I and astral body

throughout life. After death, the soul wants again and again to wake up in the body. This is something it has to learn to do without, and it will take about a third of a lifetime to do so. Sleep takes up about a third of life. The first day after you have died you'll want to go back. You'll want to do what you did the last day of your life. On the second day you'll want to do what you did the last but one day of your life, and that is how it goes on. The craving thus has to be got rid of for this third of life. You won't feel the cravings of hunger or thirst after death, but for everything you have had through your physical body. It will be like this after death. All your life you developed a love for the area around your home village. It is something you have always been seeing. And you have been seeing it through your physical body. Only people with strange beliefs will think that they'll have much more beautiful meadows, flowers and so on after death than they have here on earth. And we have to let go of all this. And because this needs to be done, we have to say that cravings continue. I think you can understand this?

Answer: Yes, indeed.

Cravings for the physical body and for life altogether continue after death, therefore. No longer hunger and thirst, for that would need a stomach. We won't have a stomach then, that will have been put into the coffin. But above all there is a craving after death still to see all the things we have seen during life.

There is something else as well. After death we'll not be able to see things rightly in the spiritual way in the world we have entered, just as an infant does not see things fully here in the physical world. This is something that has to be learned. We have to grow into the world of the spirit. The first stage after death, a third of our past life, therefore is such that we are blind and deaf to the world of the spirit but still long for the physical world. This comes after the two or three days in which the individual who has died looks back on his life, as I have told you. And it is only when he has shed these longings that he will grow into the world of the spirit and gain perceptions in the spirit. He'll no longer have the craving for the physical world then. Anyone able to understand the inner life will therefore also understand what remains of our physical life. And the things that remain are not all pleasant, of course. If someone has been always wanting to beat up other people, the craving to beat people up will remain, and he must gradually get out of the habit. These are the things one comes to understand.

In anthroposophy we always seek to understand what can be truly seen of the soul, being truly apparent. This is what it is about.

As to your other question, the one concerning Christ Jesus, we'll consider it a little bit right now, today, so that you'll not feel dissatisfied. It does mean, however, that I have to go into history first.

I have told you of all kinds of stages which the earth went through in very early times. Now the thing is like this. Conditions on earth today have at most existed for six to eight or nine thousand years, let's say 6,000 to 9,000 years. This also agrees with observations made by modern scientists, and I have mentioned this to you before. Before that, you would not have been able to go far from here and you would be in the glacier region, as it is called. Switzerland was then covered with glaciers all the way to here, in places where you can walk around today. Glaciers then flowed in valleys where rivers flow today. The Aare, the Reuss and so on, are thinned-down remnants of glacier rivers from those times.

The time when Europe was largely under ice was preceded by a time that was very different. The earth is such — though you have to think in very large spans of time for this — that its surfaces are always going up and down, rising and falling. So if this is the sea, for example [drawing on the board], with land up there, this land is floating in the sea. All land actually floats in the sea. Can you imagine this? It is not that it goes down to the bottom; the land, all lands, float in the sea. The sea is also beneath the land.

Now you'll say: 'But why does it not move around in that case, like a ship?' Let me first tell you something else. The land masses do indeed float in the sea, but imagine this is Great Britain, England [drawing on the board]. It is an island. It does indeed float in the sea, but close to Europe, and the distance does not change. Even from the modern scientific view, however, it has not always been like that, and there have been times when the water went over the land. England was then under the sea. Going across this little bit of sea you would, of course, reach bottom. So there have been times when England was beneath the sea.

The situation is actually like this. If you study the soil in England you'll find some fossilized creatures in it and they are not all the same. If you look at a bit of English soil here, and then again higher up, the fossilized animals will be quite different, and quite different again if you go even higher up. You'll find four successive layers of fossilized animals in the English soil!

Where do these fossilized animals come from? When the sea floods the land, the animals die. Their shells drop down and the animals are fossilized. If I find four different layers in a soil, the land must have been under the sea four times. It would have put down a layer each time. And looking at England we find that the land was up above and then down below again four times. England was below sea level four times, and it always rose again.

Now you may ask: 'Why does such an island, which is really floating in water, not move about like a ship?' Well, it is not held in place by the earth. If only the earth were involved, you simply cannot imagine how things would be shaken up and thrown into confusion. England would hit the Norwegian coast one day and then be moved across to America, and so on, and the countries would all be thrown into confusion if it were only a matter for the earth. But it is not just a matter for the earth, for it is the relative positions of the stars which send out the forces that keep a land mass in a particular place. It thus is not the earth which does it. It is the relative positions of the stars. And it is always possible to show that when a land mass has changed position, the relative position of the stars has changed — not the planets, of course, but the fixed stars. Someone who does not want to know about this world is just like people who say the powers of thought come from the brain. If I leave footprints in soft soil and someone coming from Mars, if you like, says the footprints have been produced by the earth, with the earth pushing the sand up or pulling it down, that is not the way it is at all, for I have pressed down the soil from outside. And the convolutions of the brain have also come from outside, from the soul's thinking. And that is also how it is with the land masses on earth. They are held in place by the relative position of the stars. And so we find that the spirit has to be seen to be not only in the human beings on earth, and on the earth altogether, but in the whole of the universe.

Now just think, gentlemen, people of earlier times actually knew these things, though in a very different way than we do today. Let me prove this to you. Several centuries before the birth of Christ a great philosopher called Plato lived in Greece.[39] He knew a great deal. He told how one of the wisest people of his nation, Solon, went to see an Egyptian once. The Egyptians were the older nation at the time, but the Greeks had more sense than we have, for though they greatly revered the Egyptians — as we shall see in a minute — they did not learn Egyptian, the ancient language of the Egyptians. The Greeks did not learn

Egyptian! Our scholars all have to learn Greek! The Greeks had more sense. We do not copy what they aimed to do; but we copy their language. Our scholars are handicapped exactly because they do not grow into the things that would come to them naturally on earth but are deflected from this by having to find their way into a very ancient language. Well, people are now trying to change this in Switzerland. When our young people wanted to study medicine, they first had their minds warped by having to learn Greek. I am not saying this because I, too, had to learn it once. I truly love the Greek language. But it should be for people to learn who want to gain something from it, not because they want to be doctors or lawyers and later forget their Greek again.

Plato told the story of Solon and the Egyptian. And this clever Egyptian said to him: 'You Greeks may be quite advanced, but you are still children, for you do not know anything about the land masses being drawn up above the sea all the time and then going down again, with the situation changing all the time.'

The ancient Egyptians thus still knew it and the Greeks no longer did. Only Plato. He did know something about the fact that there had been land out there in the Atlantic Ocean, where ships go from Europe to America today, so that there had been a land connection between the west coast of Europe and the east coast of America. But the old truths have been forgotten. And this was because knowledge was then still at a more unconscious level. We have learned to think in an abstract way, which is something we need in order to be free. For those people in the past were not free; but they did know more. And Lessing, I told you, set great store by the fact that earlier people knew more than those who came later.

And so we come to a point where we say to ourselves: 'It is true that in very early times, and because of the way they then were by nature, people knew that a spiritual principle is present all around. People knew this for quite a long time.'

There was a Roman emperor in the fourth century after Christ, for instance, whose name was Julian.[40] He was taught by people who still had some of the Asian knowledge. And Julian said that there was not one sun but three. The first sun is the physical sun, the second a sun of soul, and the third a sun of spirit. The first is visible, the other two are invisible. This is what Julian said.

Then something very strange happened. Julian has always been given a bad name in history, for he did not believe in Christianity. But he did believe in the things people knew before Christianity came. And one day, when he had to conduct a military campaign in Asia, he was murdered all of a sudden. It was a kind of assassination. But the assassination was done by people who hated him because he had still acquired the old knowledge.

You just have to remember that at that time, in earlier days, the matter was handled very differently from the way it is today. The Egyptians were terribly clever, as I've told you. But they did not have the kind of writing we have; they wrote in pictures, with a word always looking similar to what it meant. And the scribes of ancient Egypt were always told that writing was a sacred task and that they had to copy things exactly. Do you know what would happen to someone who was careless enough to make an error in writing in pictures? He would be condemned to death! Now today we'd be really surprised if someone were condemned to death for a spelling error. But human history is different from the way we think. The ancient Egyptians were indeed both wise and cruel in some respects. So there has of course been some progress in human evolution. But though writing was so sacred to them, we cannot deny that they were indeed wise in other respects and knew about things that are only gradually emerging again today in anthroposophy, in a very different way. They actually dreamt it, and we know it. It was a completely different way.

Now you see, Julian was right. It is indeed true that just as you have soul and spirit in your body, so does the sun have soul and spirit. Someone who knows the soul element will say so. He would not say that a Venus's fly-trap has a soul, for it would be nonsense to say that anything that moves in some way for a purpose also has a soul. He knows, however, that light has a soul when it shines, and moves in a soul way. This is something he perceives. And people thus knew that the sun had a living entity inside it.

Now you know we are told that Jesus of Nazareth was born in Palestine at a particular time. You see, gentlemen, Jesus of Nazareth grew up in fairly simple circumstances — we can check the things written in the Gospels today, that they are true. He was the son of a carpenter, a joiner. That is correct. He grew up in a fairly simple way. He still had a great deal of the old wisdom. And it is also true that he was able to give very good answers to the scribes and scholars when he was 12 years old. It can still happen today that a boy of 12 gives more sensible answers than a scholar whose head has been turned by scholarship. It was then apparent that he was a greatly gifted child. He continued to grow up, and when he was 30 years old something suddenly changed in him.

What happened in Jesus when he was 30 years old? When Jesus was 30 years old he suddenly understood something — he had of course been prepared for this by the great knowledge he'd had before. It was something people no longer knew at that time. Only a few unknown scholars still knew it from ancient wisdom, so that Julian was also able to discover it at a later time. He came to see, out of ancient knowledge, that the whole universe and the sun had soul and spirit. And the reality that lived in the universe filled him when he came to know it. When we know something, we do indeed have it.

In those days things had to be taught to people in images. The things I am telling you today can only be put the way they are put since the fifteenth century. Before that, people did not have these concepts. They therefore said that a dove came down and he received the holy spirit into him. The situation was, of course, that anyone able to perceive it would know that something had happened to him. It would be put in this way, and in one of the Gospels it says: 'And lo a voice from heaven saying, This is my beloved son, in whom I am well pleased.'[41] Properly translated: 'This is my beloved son; today I have born him.' It means that the event which happened in his thirtieth year was truly seen as a second birth. The birth of Jesus was just the birth of a boy who was more gifted than others, but who did not yet have this feeling in him. This was felt to be something extraordinarily important. It was the baptism in the Jordan.

There was something once that was a real problem to me. You do get such problems in science, gentlemen! One had the four Gospels, as you know, the Gospels of Matthew, Mark, Luke and John. And of course today everyone knows that they contradict each other. When you read the genealogy of Jesus at the beginning of Matthew's Gospel and compare it with the genealogy in Luke's Gospel, they are contradictory. People will say: 'They do not agree.' But they don't give it any further thought. At most they'll say: 'This was invented by one person, and this by another; one of them simply invented something different from the other, and we therefore have the contradiction.'

But that is not how it is. It is like this. Goethe, for example, said of himself: 'I have my stature from my father,' meaning he looked rather like him:

I have my stature from my father,
The serious approach to life;
My cheerfulness comes from my mother,
As does delight in making up stories.[42]

Well, perhaps Goethe was not yet able to make up stories when he was three; it may have been something he was able to do when he was nine. Then he had to say: 'Right, delight in making up stories comes from my mother; it has come to me from my mother.'

I am telling you this because it will help you understand how my problem of the contradictions in the Gospels was resolved.

I first of all took these two Gospels, the Gospel of Matthew and the Gospel of Luke. Now if one does not just carelessly say they are inventions, no one can know why the two are contradictory. I therefore did a spiritual scientific investigation to discover what lies behind it and found that it was not just one boy who was born but that two Jesus children were born. Both were called Jesus. That need not really surprise us, for if a boy is called Joseph in Austria, no one will be surprised if another boy, born at the same time, is also called Joseph. It need not surprise us if two boys are called Seppl (short for Joseph) or Francis. And so one need not be surprised that two boys were both called Jesus at that time. Two boys were in fact born who were both called Jesus.[43] They lived together up to their twelfth year. And then something strange happened. Because they had lived together, the gifts which one of them had suddenly appeared in the other. Just as a son can inherit gifts from his mother, so did the one Jesus child inherit the gifts of the other, for instance. And the Jesus child whose gifts the other one had inherited did not continue to live, he died at 12 years of age; he died soon after. One of them thus remained, and because he was deeply touched by the fact that the other one was departing from this life, the wisdom of the other boy came alight in him. And it was only because of this that he could impress the scholars with his brilliance.

The parents could have said: 'Where does he get it from?' An explanation can be found if we accept that the soul principle also has an influence. And such soul influences simply exist. The one Jesus child did not have wisdom until he reached his twelfth year. The other one died, and his wisdom had come to the other Jesus child, partly due to the shock of the other boy dying, partly because they had been friends. And this Jesus went through the baptism in the Jordan. The truth is that two Jesus children were born, not one. One of them died in his twelfth year, and the other suddenly woke up from the shock and then had the wisdom of the other boy.

And you then find that one of the evangelists, Matthew, wrote of the childhood of the one Jesus child, whilst the other, Luke, wrote of the other Jesus child. The two therefore are in agreement. I have not thought this up. It is the result of research work. And I am therefore speaking of two Jesus children because I have knowledge that the others do not have.

You can see from this that in the science of the spirit we apply the same principles as in natural science, saying that if there are causes, effects will also show themselves. We do not simply say: 'Well, two people simply invented something. The one Jesus child, in Matthew, is an invention, and the other Jesus child, in Luke, is an invention.' At the time when the Gospels of Matthew and Luke were written, there was no thought of inventing things like this. People spoke in images; but they did not invent things, for they took things very seriously, so seriously that when a scribe wrote something that was not correct he would have been condemned to death a few centuries earlier in Egypt. We should not just carelessly say that people in earlier times invented things. They put it in images. But it would never have entered their heads to invent anything. Only an ignorant person would say that the Gospels of Matthew and Luke are probably inventions. Yet this is what present-day scholars and theologians are saying. They cannot help themselves but have to admit that there are contradictions. But if one knows that there were two Jesus children, one of them the Jesus child of Matthew's Gospel, the other the Jesus child of Luke's Gospel, the matter is made clear in the best possible way.

Now there comes Mr Hauer. He is a visiting lecturer at Tübingen University and elsewhere. He's against anthroposophy. Today it does not profit you to speak for anthroposophy, but it does certainly profit you to speak against anthroposophy. Mr Hauer has therefore come along and found this to be something strange and peculiar. Well, gentlemen, it certainly is strange and peculiar because no one has discovered it before. It is of course peculiar for me to say that there was not one Jesus child but two, and one of them died in his twelfth year. Of course it is peculiar. It is not at all surprising that it is peculiar. But it is peculiar only because it is something no one else has said before. Because of this, Hauer finds it all strange and peculiar. You find this on every page of his book.

On the other hand you will find this: 'Well now, Steiner does not say anything that has not been known before.' Well, gentlemen, Mr Hauer finds anything he did not know before peculiar. He complains about it. On the basis of things he has read here and there—the old wisdom has existed, and you will of course find it written down everywhere today; I do not read it up here and there but it comes together—he concludes: 'Well, Steiner is not saying anything people have not been saying before.' That is how you find yourself at the mercy of these people. If something has to be said somewhere they will say: 'He is not saying anything new.' To write a book on geometry I would of course have to include the Pythagorean theorem. Pythagoras discovered this 600 years before Christ was born. I may have a number of new things in the book, and I must also have the Pythagorean theorem. I'd prove it in a slightly different way today, but it would be there in the book. Surely people cannot complain if something that has been forgotten is found again! And so it is true that many of the things which are today, of course, said in the science of the spirit can be found in the works of the ancient Gnostics, who were the writers in an earlier time. They will have put it differently, for it was a different situation then. Gnostics still existed at the time when Christ was on earth, and also after that. They wrote down such ancient wisdom, but this did not come from science but from ancient knowledge, so this was different from anthroposophy. People will compare what is written in anthroposophical works with Gnostic works. It is a little bit the way it is also found in the work of the Gnostics, because it is true. And these people will then say: 'Well, he's not saying anything that the others did not also say.' But when it comes to the two Jesus children, Hauer is, of course, unable to say: 'Here Steiner has discovered something which the others also knew.' In this case, he simply has no notion of anyone ever knowing this before.

The whole book—I've not yet cut the pages—but anything I have seen of it so far is teeming with this kind of contradiction. If you compare one page with another, you find nothing really hangs together. But that is what modern scholars do. On the one hand they say: 'Others have said this before, many times.' And on the other hand they'll say: 'He's not saying anything new. We already knew all about it.' Well, if they've known all about it already, why then are they complaining? And on the other hand, if there is anything they did not know before they find it unbelievable.

But you see, when I had found this, truly finding it entirely by means of spiritual research, that there were two Jesus children who lived together until their twelfth year, I knew no more than that it is a fact. Then one day in Turin we saw a painting.[44] This painting is rather unusual. It shows the mother of Jesus and two boys. One of them was not John, for we all know what John is like from all the paintings that show both Jesus and John. The two boys in the picture look fairly similar and yet also not similar. It is quite evident that these are two young friends. If one has already discovered that there were two Jesus children, one will realize what this painting tells us. It was painted at a relatively late date; but an Italian painter put two Jesus children in a painting at a time when people still knew that there had been two Jesus children.

If Hauer knew that this had still been the case, from ancient knowledge, he would now say: 'It simply means that Steiner has seen the painting in Turin.' He would say he had known it all along. And he would go on to say: 'Steiner is not telling us anything new; he always only says things we've known anyway.' That's how people are.

It really is quite a terrible thing to consider the contradictions people come up with, evidently silly things, to fight anthroposophy. On the one hand the things I say are supposed to be invented. All right, let us assume it is an invention of mine. But the same person then surely cannot say in the same book: 'What he says is nothing new!' He insists that I have invented those things and objects to my doing so. And then he goes on to say that others have known them before. What these people do is simply crack-brained. Yet if you truly approach the Christ event and investigate it the way you normally investigate facts, it becomes very clear that the Jesus child's tremendous gifts had come from give-and-take between the two boys.

Let me prove to you that such give-and-take is possible,

with other people not realizing that it is taking place. You see — I am going to tell you of one such case, but there are many such cases — there was a little girl once who had older brothers and sisters. Those brothers and sisters had learned to talk quite properly. The little girl did not learn to talk properly at first. When she did start to talk — which was a bit later than with other children — she was talking, true enough. But she spoke a language which no adult could understand. She'd say 'papazzo', for instance, and when she used this word she meant the dog. And so she invented her own names for all the animals. These are scientific facts. Those names cannot be found anywhere else.

After a time the girl had a new little brother. And the little brother very soon learned that language from his sister. And they would talk to one another in that language. The little brother died when he was about 12 years old, and the girl got out of the habit of that language and learned to talk like everyone else. She married later and was a perfectly ordinary middle-class woman. She'd tell people the story. It was something she had gone through herself. A fact. The two children communicated in that language, talking to one another in a language which no one else understood. Gentlemen, that may be the greatest wisdom! Only those two understood one another and had an understanding about this.

You can see from this how one individual is influenced by another. So why should it not have been the case that the one Jesus child, who died when he was 12, knew something which no one else understood? If you know the facts, you see it again and again.

Nothing is said here, therefore, that cannot also be most eminently scientific. People who will not accept that it is scientific don't always get their facts together. Someone who knows that such things happen, that two children speak a language which no adult can understand, and share something in mind and spirit in which the adults have no part, will understand everything I am saying about the two Jesus children up to their twelfth year. And it is not surprising that this was an unusual thing. It does not happen every day. And it only happened once in world history in the form in which it happened then—with illumination then coming to this individual when he was 30 years old.

Now you see, there the Christ story becomes true science, true insight. And here one cannot help oneself; it changes of its own accord when insight is gained.

Now you might say: 'All right, then, Jesus had been illuminated when he was 12 years old by the other boy, the one who died. But when he was 30, he had again suddenly become a different person.' The evangelist put it in words by writing: 'A dove came down upon him from heaven.'[45]

Yes, gentlemen, the fact is that he did become another person. So what happened there? I have told you that when a child is born you first of all have an embryo. The spirit of the universe has to influence this embryo. No wonder that the spirit of the universe has an influence when it even has an influence on the island that is England, as we have seen. The event that happened for Jesus in his thirtieth year cannot be explained if we just consider the earth. Just as a human being comes into existence on fertilization, with one thing influencing another, so did the whole universe have an influence on the 30-year-old Jesus at that time, fertilizing him with a soul and spirit principle, and he then became Jesus Christ, or, better, Christ Jesus. For what does it mean? Christ is the name for someone who has been illuminated. And Jesus was a common first name in Palestine, just as people are called Seppl in Austria today, meaning Joseph, or in Switzerland, and so on, where you find such names in every family. Many were called Jesus, therefore, and he was called the Christ because there had been this illumination.

Yes, gentlemen, if you read my book *Christianity as*

Mystical Fact,[46] you will find proof there that this illumination had already been brought about artificially before that for some people, only to a lesser degree. They would then be called the wise ones of the mysteries. The difference between people trained to have the greatest wisdom in dim antiquity, the difference between them and Jesus Christ was that those wise ones of the mysteries were taught by others in schools which were then called the mysteries. In Jesus it happened of its own accord. It therefore was a different process.

In the ancient mysteries, people who achieved the greatest wisdom were known as 'Christ'. It is just like today when you need not be surprised if someone who has been studying until he was 25 — before that he was plain Joseph Miller, now he is suddenly Dr Miller. That is how people became 'Christ' in the old mysteries, though not exactly in such a simple way; for you can of course be an absolute nincompoop and still have the doctor title at 25. That was not possible in the ancient mysteries; there it was deep, deep wisdom. Then people became 'Christ'. It was the title given to the wisest people, just as today the doctor title is given after some degree of study. Only in those days, if things went the way they should, it was genuine wisdom. And this happened of its own accord in the case of the Christ. It means that something which was otherwise given from the earth, by people, was given from the wide expanse of the cosmos. It only happened once. World history then took another turn. And it cannot be denied by anyone, not even someone who is not a Christian, that world history took a different turn then.

The Romans did not take account of it, for they did not know it. Christianity was founded over yonder in Asia by Christ Jesus. At the same time the Romans progressed from an ancient republic to being an empire, and they persecuted the Christians. The Christians had to make catacombs for themselves down below, underground. There they thought about the nature of their Christianity. Up above ground, what did people do there? They had circuses, tying human beings, their slaves, to pillars and burning them to provide a spectacle for the people sitting in the circus. That was up above ground. And down below in the catacombs the Christians lived their wisdom, religion, which at that time was for people who lived in slavery. Religion simply means union — *religere*, to bind, to unite. The Christians had their religion below ground.

And what happened a few centuries later? The Romans were no longer there in the old way. No one was any more looking at burning people just for pleasure; that had gone. The Christians had taken their place.

And that is also how it will be. People who talk like Dr Hauer today, the man you mentioned, will without doubt be swept away. And something which today has to be active in catacombs — not physically so, but in spirit — will have its effect. But you have to understand that it is genuine science; and how it annoys people who are not learning much today that something like this is coming up!

I'll be able to take this further when I am back again. But I think you will have got a general idea of the way in which this is going.

On the Christ, Ahriman and Lucifer and their relationship to man

Good morning, gentlemen, have you thought of something we might discuss today?

Question: Perhaps Dr Steiner would say something about the true nature of the Christ, Ahriman and Lucifer in relationship to human beings?

Rudolf Steiner: For this we must consider the true nature of man from another point of view, otherwise it might sound like superstition to you. Basing myself on the things we have already been discussing, let me now say the following.

You see, gentlemen, today the general thinking is that the human being is the same all the way through. That is not how it is, for the human being is really all the time in a condition where he comes alive and dies again. We don't only come to life when we are born and die when we die. We are all the time dying and coming alive again, as I have also told you on other occasions.

Now if we look at the head, for instance, the inside of the head really consists completely of what we call 'nerve substance' inside. As you know, the nerves are otherwise just threads running through the body, but the head is all nerve inside. We might show it like this in a drawing [Fig. 27]: head, forehead; there head is all nerve inside, a thick mass of nerve matter. Some of this nerve matter also goes down the spinal marrow, and then the nerve threads go all through the body. Matter that occurs only in threads throughout the body is thus a uniform mass in the head. That is the nerve mass.

If you were to look at the inside of the human belly, you

Fig. 27

still have many nerves in there. There you have the solar plexus, as it is called. There's still a lot of nerve in there. But in the arms and hands and in the legs and feet the nerves are mere threads.

If you now look at something else again, the blood vessels, you'll find that they are fairly delicate in the head. On the other hand the blood vessels are particularly well developed in the heart region; and there are also thick blood vessels in the limbs. We are therefore able to say that on the one hand we have the nerve system, and on the other the blood system.

Now the situation is that we are born again out of the blood every day and every hour. Blood always means renewal. If we only had blood in us, therefore, we would be like creatures that grow all the time, getting bigger, creatures that are fresh and new, and so on. But you see, gentlemen, if we were nothing but nerve, consisting only of nerves, we would all the time be tired and worn; we would really be dying all the time. We therefore have two opposite principles in us — the nervous system that makes us get old all the time, actually handing us over to death all the time, and the blood system which is connected with the nutrition system and lets us grow young all the time, and so on.

We can take this matter, of which I have just spoken, further. As you know, some people change in old age in such a way that we have to say they are calcified. Calcification, sclerosis develops. When people's arteries get furred up, as we say, when the walls of the blood vessels calcify, people easily reach a point where they can no longer move so well. And if the calcification gets really severe, one has a stroke, as we say. One has a stroke. This stroke, which people get, simply means that their blood vessels calcify and no longer stand up to the strain.

What has come over someone who calcifies, who grows sclerotic? You see, it is as if the walls of his blood vessels want to turn into nerves. That is the strange thing. The nerves have to die all the time. The nerves have to be in a condition throughout life, as it were, in which the blood vessels must never be. The blood vessels have to be fresh. The nerves must all the time be inclined to die off. If someone's nerves get too soft, not sufficiently calcified, if I may put it like this, he'll go mad. So you see, nerves must not be like blood vessels and blood vessels must not be like nerves.

This really compels us to say that man has two principles in him. One is the nerve principle. It really makes him old all the time. We really get a little bit older all the time from morning to evening. During the night this freshens up again, something that comes from the blood. And that is how it goes all the time, like the pendulum swing of a clock—grow old, grow young, grow old, grow young. Of course, if we are awake from morning to evening, we'll get older; and when we sleep from evening till morning, we'll get younger again. But there's always a little bit left over. The night does improve the situation; but a little bit of every day's getting older is left over. And when the sum of this gets big enough, the person will truly die. That is the way it is. So we have two things in the human being that work in opposite directions—growing old and growing young.

Now we can also look at this with regard to the soul. I have so far spoken of the body. You see, if getting young grows too powerful in a person, he'll get pleurisy or pneumonia. The point is that things which are really quite good, which are excellent within their limits, become illness if they get too powerful. Sickness in human beings simply means that something which they always need is getting too powerful. A temperature develops when the getting-young process grows much too powerful in us. We cannot cope with this. We begin to be too fresh with the whole of our body. We then have a temperature, or pleurisy, or pneumonia.

Now we can also look at this from the point of view of the soul. You see, people can also dry up in their souls, or else get into the kind of state which in the physical body would be a temperature. People have some character traits—we don't like to hear about them, because so many people have them today—where they become pedantic, become philistines. Philistines do exist. You get to be a pedantic philistine. And if you are a teacher, someone who should be really fresh and lively, you get to be as dry as dust. And you see, this is the same as when our blood vessels calcify and dry up. We can also dry up in our souls. And on the other hand we may also grow soft in our souls. This means we get to be zealous, mystical—or theosophists! What is it that we want in that case? We don't want to think properly. We want to reach out to all the world with our powers of fantasy and not think properly. This is the same as the temperature you get in the body. To become a mystic, a theosophist, is to develop a temperature in your soul.

But we must always have the two things in us. We are quite unable to have insight unless we use fantasy, and we are quite unable to somehow bring things together in our work unless we are a little bit pedantic, keeping records of all kinds of things, and so on. Too much of this, and we are pedantic, we are philistines. Getting the balance right means the soul is as it should be.

The point is that there is always something or other that has to be at the right level in a human being. If it gets too powerful it will make us sick in body or soul.

It is also like this with the spirit, gentlemen. We cannot sleep for ever but have to wake up occasionally. Just think of the jolt it is to wake up. Just imagine the way it is with sleep. You lie there, knowing nothing about the world around you. If you're having a good sleep, someone may even come and tickle you and you won't wake up. Now think of the difference when you wake up, seeing everything around you. That is a big difference. Now when you wake up—yes, we must have the power to wake up in us; but if it is too great, if one is always waking up, if one can't sleep at all, for example, the power to wake up is too strong in us.

Now there are also people who cannot ever wake up properly. Some people are always in a dim, dreamy state of mind, wanting to sleep all the time. They cannot wake up. We need the ability to go to sleep properly; yet this ability should not be too great. Otherwise we sleep for ever and never wake up at all.

We are thus able to say that different conditions can be seen at three levels in human beings. The first level is physical. On the one hand we have our nervous system.

This shows a constant tendency to harden, to calcify. So we say:

physically	hardening
	calcification

You see, you are all of you at an age — with the exception of just one who is sitting there among you — that you must have your nervous system a little bit calcified. For if you still had the nervous system today the way you had it when you were six months old, you would all be mad. You can't have that kind of soft nervous system any more. People who are mad have a child-level nervous system. So we have to have the power to harden, to calcify, in us. And on the other hand we must have the power to soften, to grow younger. The two powers need to be in balance.

physically	hardening	softening
	calcification	growing young

If we look at the soul level, we are able to say that the soul equivalent of hardening is pedantry, being philistine, materialistic, with a dry intellect.

All this needs to be understood. We have to be a bit of a philistine or we'd be madcaps. We have to be a bit pedantic or we would not keep our things in proper order. We'd hang our jackets in the stove or in the chimney rather than in the wardrobe. So it's not a bad thing to be a bit of a philistine and a bit pedantic, but of course not too much of it. We also have the power of fantasy, the power to be dreamers, mystics, theosophists. If all of these get too much, these powers, we will be dreamers, we'll live in fantasies. This must not happen. But on the other hand we also should not be completely without fantasy.

I once knew someone who hated anything by way of fantasy. He never went to the theatre, for instance, let alone the opera, for he'd say none of it was true. He had no fantasy at all. But someone who has no fantasy at all will be very dry, sneaking through life, and not a real, proper human being. So again things must not go to extremes.

in the soul	pedantry	fantasy
	philistinism	dreaminess
	materialism	mysticism
	dry intellect	theosophy

If we now look at the spiritual side of things, we have the power of hardening in waking up. Waking up, we firmly take hold of the body, using our limbs. And the power which at the physical level causes softening, getting younger, we have here on going to sleep. Then we sink into dreams. We no longer have our bodies in hand.

in the spirit	waking up	going to sleep

We can say that human beings are constantly in danger of falling into the one extreme or the other, either becoming subject to too much softening or going into excessive hardening.

If you have a magnet you know it attracts iron. We speak of two kinds of magnetism in the magnet. And that is true. We have positive magnetism and negative magnetism. The one attracts the magnetic needle, the other repels it. They are opposites.

You'll agree that when it comes to physical, bodily things, we are not afraid to call things by their names. We need names. I have now described something to you in body, soul and spirit which every one of you can perceive for himself, something we always see, and about which you can all be quite clear in your minds. But we need names. When we have positive magnetism, we have to understand that this is not the iron; it is something in the iron. There is something invisible in the iron.

Someone who will not admit that there is something

invisible in the piece of iron will say: 'You are daft! Iron is supposed to have a magnetism in it? This is a horseshoe. I use it to shoe my horse.' I think you'll agree that someone who'll not admit that there is something invisible in the iron and uses it just to shoe his horse is an idiot. You can also use this horseshoe for quite a different purpose if it has magnetism inside it.

Now you see, something invisible, something we cannot perceive with the senses, is present in the hardening process. And this invisible, supersensible principle, which one can observe if one has the gift for it, is called ahrimanic. The powers that want to make the human being into a kind of corpse all the time are ahrimanic. If only the ahrimanic powers were there, we would all the time turn into corpses, we would be pedantic, human beings turned to stone. We would wake up all the time and be unable to sleep.

The powers that soften us and make us younger, taking us into fantasy, are the luciferic powers. We need the luciferic powers so that we may not become living corpses. But if only luciferic powers were present, well, then we would be children for the whole of our lives. The luciferic powers are needed in the world, so that we do not become old people at three years of age. The ahrimanic powers are needed in the world, so that we do not remain children for ever. These two opposing powers must be present in the human being.

	ahrimanic	luciferic
physically	hardening	softening
	calcification	growing young
in the soul	pedantry	fantasy
	philistinism	dreaminess
	materialism	mysticism
	dry intellect	theosophy
in the spirit	waking up	going to sleep

Now it is important that these two powers must be in balance. How is the balance held? Nothing of these two powers should gain the upper hand.

You see, it is now the year 1923, as you know. This whole time from the beginning of the century until 1923 has really been such that humanity is in danger of falling prey to the ahrimanic powers. Just consider—we are educated in an ahrimanic way today, unless there is a science of the spirit. Just think—our children go to primary school where they have to learn things that must seem very odd to them, things that cannot possibly interest them. I have mentioned this before. They have always seen their father. He looks like this—hair, ears, eyes—and then they are supposed to learn this: *f a t h e r* [writing on the board] is their father. It is something quite alien to them. And that is how it is with all the things children are supposed to learn initially in primary school. They are not the least bit interested.

And that is, of course, the reason why we must establish sensible schools again, where children may first of all learn things that would interest them. If the teaching were to continue the way it is done at the moment, people would grow old very early, for it is ahrimanic. This makes people old. The way children are educated at school today—it is all ahrimanic. The way it has been in these 1900 years is that the whole of human evolution has gone in the ahrimanic direction. It was different before.

If you go back to, let us say, the time from the year 8000 BC to the turning-point of time, things were different then. People then faced the danger of not being able to grow old. They did not have schools in those early times the way we have today. Schools were only for people who had already reached a respectable age and were meant to be real scholars. They had schools for those people. There were no schools for children then. They would learn from life. They would learn the things they saw. And so they did not have schools, nor was any kind of effort made to teach the children anything that was alien to them. The danger with this was that people might become utterly luciferic, dreamers, in short, luciferic. And they did. Much wisdom existed in those early times, as I have told you. But this luciferic principle had to be controlled, otherwise they might have gone on all day telling each other ghost stories! That was something people were particularly fond of then.

We are thus able to say that in very early times, from about the year 8000 BC to the turning-point of time, it was a luciferic age. And then came an ahrimanic age.

Let us take a look at the luciferic age. You see, the people who were the scholars in those early times had some problems. At that time scholars would live in places that were like towers. The tower of Babylon about which the Bible tells us was one of those buildings. That is where the scholars lived. These scholars would say: 'Yes, of course, we are fortunate. For fantasy also wants to take over our minds. We always want to go into ghostly, luciferic things. But we have our instruments. With them we look into the stars and see how they move. This puts a rein on our fantasy.' You see, if I look at a star and want it to go a particular way, it won't do it. So then my own fantasy is reined in.

The scholars therefore knew that they could use the phenomena of the world to keep a rein on their fantasy. Or they would have instruments for physics. They would know: 'If I were to think that burning a very small piece of wood will give me a huge fire, I can imagine this, but when I do it in reality the small piece of wood will only give me a small fire.'

That was really the purpose of those ancient schools — to keep a rein on the lively powers of imagination those people had. And their problem was that they would say: 'Yes, but there are all the other people who cannot be scholars.' And so they made their teachings public, sometimes honestly so and sometimes in a dishonest way. These are the ancient religious teachings, and they were certainly based on great knowledge. Only it would sometimes happen, of course, that the priests went astray. And the result is that the dishonest teachings—the honest ones have largely been lost—have come down to posterity. That was the way in which a rein was kept on the luciferic element.

As to how things are in the ahrimanic way—this you know. Present-day science is going more and more ahrimanic. The whole of our science today is really designed to make us all dried up. For in this science people really only know the physical world, which is the calcified, material world. And this is the ahrimanic element in our present civilization.

Between the two is the principle which we call Christian in the true sense. You see, gentlemen, people do not really know the truly Christian spirit today. If you take the element known as 'Christian' in this world today, this is indeed something we would have to fight, that is obvious.

But the spirit of whom I also said a few things the last time we met, who was born at the turning-point of time and lived for 33 years—this individual was not the way people say he was. His true aim was to teach the whole of humanity the things that will make it possible to create a balance between the ahrimanic and luciferic elements. And to be Christian is indeed to look for the balance between the ahrimanic and luciferic elements. You really cannot be Christian the way people often say it is supposed to be.

What does it mean, for example, to be Christian in a physical sense? To be Christian in a physical way is to learn things about the human being. A human being can fall ill. He gets pleurisy. What does it mean when we say he gets pleurisy? It means there is too much of the luciferic element in him. If I know this, that there is too much of the luciferic in him, I have to say: 'If I have some scales [Fig. 28] and they

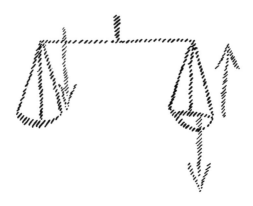

Fig. 28

shoot up too much on this side, I have to take away some weights. If it goes down too much here, I must add weights there. And so I now say to myself that when someone has pleurisy the luciferic element is too powerful and the ahrimanic too weak. I have to add something ahrimanic to balance it out.

So let us assume I say to myself, quite rightly: 'This person has pleurisy; how can I help him?' I take a piece of birch wood, let us say. Birch wood grows actively in spring. And birch wood is something really good, especially the part near the bark; the bark has excellent powers of growth. I kill these by making the birch wood into charcoal. So what have I made of that fresh birch wood that was always growing young again? I made it into birch charcoal, something ahrimanic. And I then make the birch charcoal into a powder[47] and give this to the person who has too much of the luciferic element in him with his pleurisy. I have then added the ahrimanic element to the luciferic of which he has too much.

You see, I have made things balance out. Just as I have to add something when the scales go up too much on one side, so I have added birch charcoal when there is too much of the luciferic element in that pleurisy. I made the birch wood mineral by turning it into charcoal. It has been made ahrimanic.

Or let us assume someone gets to look so tired, inactive, that I have to say to myself: 'He'll have a stroke next.' He has too much of the ahrimanic element in him. I then have to put something luciferic into him, to balance things out. What am I going to do in this case?

Now you see if I have a plant—there's the root [Fig. 29]. You know the root is hard. It contains many salts. That is not luciferic. The stem and the leaves are not luciferic either. But if I go higher up I come to a scented, powerfully scented flower. The scent wants to escape, just as fantasy wants to take wing. Otherwise I'd not be able to smell it. I then take the juice of the flower.[48] That is luciferic. I give it in a suitable way and so balance out the ahrimanic element, and I can cure the person.

What is done in modern medicine? In modern medicine, things are tried out. A chemist one day discovers acetyl-phenetidin.[49] I need not tell you what it is; it is a complex

Fig. 29

substance. People now take this to a hospital. There they have, say, 30 patients. All 30 patients are given acetyl-phenetidin, their temperatures taken and recorded, and if there's any result the substance is considered medicinal.

But people have no idea at all as to what is really happening in the human body. We cannot look inside the human body. It is only if we know that pleurisy means there's too much of the luciferic element and one has to add something ahrimanic, or that a stroke means there's too much of the ahrimanic element and one has to add something luciferic — then that is the right way. This is something humanity lacks today. The human race is not Christian enough in this sense, because the Christian element creates the balance. You see, I am showing you why purely physical healing can be something Christian. It is Christian because a balance is sought.

You see, this is also what I wanted to show in the wooden figure which is to be set up in the building.[50] Up above is Lucifer, the luciferic element, all the things that are feverish, fantasy, going to sleep in human beings. Lower down is everything that wants to harden, the ahrimanic element. And between the two is the Christ.

It is this which helps us to discover what we should do — in medicine, in science, in sociology and everywhere. And it is part of being human today that we understand that human nature has both luciferic and ahrimanic elements in it.

But what do people understand of these things? A pastor who was very famous in Basel and beyond, his name was Frohnmeyer,[51] once gave a lecture. He did not take the trouble to go and look at the figure, but he had read in someone else's work — who may not have seen it either, but just copied from someone else again — that a figure is being made here, luciferic at the top, the Christ in the middle, and ahrimanic down below. It is three figures, one above the other, and, as you know, there are in fact even more of them. Ahriman twice, Lucifer also twice over. This man Frohnmeyer, however, knew it so well that he wrote: 'Steiner is producing something quite terrible out there in Dornach—a Christ figure that shows luciferic traits up above and animal-like traits down below.'

Well, the Christ figure has no luciferic traits at all but a completely human head. But he got it mixed up. He thought it was a Christ figure that has luciferic features up above and animal-like characteristics down below. In actual fact the Christ figure is not at all finished yet down below, it is still a block of wood!

That is how this Christian pastor seeking the truth has described the matter, and the whole world now says it must be true, for after all it is a pastor who has written it. It is difficult to cope with this if people do not want to understand, do not want to grasp things. They always run to the pastors because they believe what they say. You have here an example of falsehood being told, an example that is so miserable that one simply cannot think of anything worse.

And these people do have strange views. Pastor Frohnmeyer has written this. At the time when he wrote it, Dr Boos was still here at the Goetheanum.[52] As you know, Dr Boos does tend to go at things a bit with a cudgel. You may have your own views as to whether one should swing a cudgel or a hand-brush. The hand-brush is softer, more luciferic, a cudgel is hard, more ahrimanic. So the question is, which should one use? Well, he told Frohnmeyer the truth, telling him the truth more with a cudgel, as it were.[53] So who gets a letter from Frohnmeyer? I do! I get a long letter from Dr Frohnmeyer in which he asks me to get Dr Boos not to be so rude to Dr Frohnmeyer.[54]

Now just think what kind of ideas people have. It is hard to believe what kind of ideas they have. They speak ill of someone, as I have told you, and then they turn to one, asking one to proceed against someone who is putting the matter straight.

This is the problem. The public, especially the middle class public, are not inclined to make the least effort to see things for themselves but simply accept what they are told. It must be right because this is someone who holds an official position. And this is why our civilization is so tremendously frivolous and so mean in many things.

The situation is that the whole way of thinking people have today must get on to a track where it is possible to see again that all this talk about Christian things will not do. We have to be objective about it. We have to know, therefore, that medicine can be Christian if we know the following, for instance. Let us say someone shows quite clearly that people who have regularly been eating sugar, perhaps even as children, get cancer of the liver—this means the liver turns ahrimanic. We then have to know what to use to treat it, and that is the corresponding luciferic element.[55] Just as we can tell the difference between hot and cold, so we must tell the difference between becoming luciferic and becoming ahrimanic. You know that if one's limbs have grown stiff, one has become ahrimanic. Hot compresses, warm cloths put on them will be the luciferic element to counteract this. And so we really have to know in all areas, and in all situations, what is the matter with a person. And then medicine will be Christian.

Education, the school system, must also become Christian. This means we have to teach in such a way that the children do not turn into old people in their earliest youth. So we must let them start at school with things that are familiar to them, in which they are interested, and so on.

You see, if we take the matter in this way, then using such terms as ahrimanic, luciferic, Christian has nothing superstitious about it but is completely scientific. And that is indeed what it is.

How did the historical evolution go? Well, you know, there was a time from the earliest Christian times until the twelfth, thirteenth centuries, and even the fourteenth century, when Christians were not allowed to read the Bible. It was forbidden to read the New Testament. Only priests were allowed to read it. The faithful in general were not allowed to read it. Why? Well, it was in fact because the clergy knew that the Bible has to be read in the right way. The Bible was created at a time when people did not think the way people do today; they still thought in images. And so one has to read the Bible in the right way. If people were to read the Bible without being properly prepared for this, they would discover that there are four Gospels in it, the Gospel of Matthew, the Gospel of Mark, the Gospel of Luke and the Gospel of John. These actually contradict each other. Why do they contradict each other? Well, gentlemen, you have to understand this the right way. Anyone who is even halfways not a fool would have realized that they contradicted each other even in the fourth or fifth century. Of course they contradict one another.

But just imagine I have taken a frontal photo of Mr Burle and show it to all of you. Well, you'll all recognize him from his picture. Then someone comes along and takes a photograph from the side, so that one sees the profile. I'd show you this and you'd all say: 'That's not Mr Burle, he looks quite different; you've got to see him from in front, then he looks like that. But the picture you are showing me that was taken from the side—that's not Mr Burle!' Well, it is Mr Burle, but we see him from two different angles. And if I were to take a photo of him from behind you'd certainly say: 'But he does have a nose as well, and not just hair!' But that is because of the different angles.

Now if we 'photograph' spiritual events from different sides, they will also look different. One simply has to know that the Gospels were written from four different points of view. They therefore have to contradict each other, just as a picture of Mr Burle looks different if it is taken from the front, from the side or from the back.

Now, however, a time has come when people have said: 'No such thing! To prepare before reading the Gospels! We don't prepare for anything any more today. We let ourselves be prepared at school; there we let ourselves be broken in. But once we've been broken in, once we are beyond the age of 14 or 15 or so, then there's nothing to prepare any more, then we have to understand everything.' Well, that's the general view today.

So why should this not also go so far that people see the Goetheanum and see it to be a place where no children go to be prepared but really old fellows with bald heads—they still want to be prepared. That must be a house of fools! You see, that's what they say, for they cannot imagine that people still want to learn. That's the way things are today. And we have to be clear in our minds that to read something like the Gospels we really have to prepare for this first, for it is meant to be in images. You know, anyone wanting to read something written in Chinese today would first have to learn the script. To take the Gospels just the way they are written would of course be nonsense, just as Chinese writing is all scribbles unless one is able to look at it the right way. But when one understands these things rightly, one discovers that with anything Christian it is always a matter of: 'You must learn to find the right balance between the ahrimanic and luciferic elements, and not let one side of the scale rise and the other go down.'

And so we anthroposophists are also not ashamed to speak of the Christian element in this sense. In anthroposophy it is made very clear that being Christian does not mean having the name of Christ on one's lips all the time, and so on. One of the reproaches directed at anthroposophy is that so little is said about the Christ. But I always say:

'You see, the name of Christ is not used all the time in anthroposophy because the Ten Commandments are taken seriously. And you talk such a lot of the Christ because you do not even know the commandment that you shall not use the Lord's name in vain.'

When a pastor preaches in a Christian church today, the name of the Christ is on his lips all the time. It should only be used if one truly understands what it is about. And this, you see, is the difference with anthroposophy, which is intended to be truly Christian, not superstitious or sanctimonious, but truly scientific, and in these terms indeed wholly scientific. And so the event that came between the earlier luciferic and the later ahrimanic times, the event that happened in Palestine, is in anthroposophy considered to be the key event in world history.

When people rightly understand once again what happened on this earth in that event, they will really find themselves again, as we might put it. Today people are really quite beyond themselves with their utterly external science. We'll talk more about this when we meet at 9 o'clock next Wednesday. This is what I wanted to say in reply to your question. I think it is possible to understand it all.

The death, resurrection and ascension of the Christ

Question: *Might we hear some more about Jesus Christ as a person?*
Rudolf Steiner: You see, gentlemen, the question has been asked at the right moment, and so we'll consider it today. Let me say right away that only those of you who have been coming for some time will understand all of it. The gentlemen who have come for the first time today will need time to find their way into the things we are discussing.

The question I have been given and which we are going to discuss concerns the Christ as an individual who lived for 33 years and then died.
Question: *'On this day he rose from the grave, he rose from the dead.' How could this be, and where did this individual gain the might and the power? And then you would perhaps be so kind as to speak of his ascension after 40 days.*

As it is just the right time of the year, I am going to speak about it the way it really happened. We have already been considering the other aspects. But, as I said, only those of you who have been coming for some time will fully understand it. The others will also come to understand, I am sure, if we get together here quite a few times.

Now you see, the first thing is that the whole business about the person of the Christ and what happened to him was relatively unknown in the times that followed immediately after the event. You should not think, the way it is generally thought today, that the events connected with the person of Jesus in Palestine became known throughout the world in an instant. That's not how it was. The situation is that at the time when the Christ Jesus went through his destiny there was the Roman Empire, a world empire, and Palestine was part of this powerful Roman Empire.

As you know, we still have a rather unfortunate legacy from the Roman Empire, and that is Roman law, as it is called. You may know that law studies at university take a very long time, for the students have to study Roman law. This had been thought up at a time when social conditions were very different, and so Roman law has of course become something that is no longer suitable in our own time. But justice is still dispensed today according to Roman law.

This, then, is a legacy from Roman times. We have various other things as well; but this one legacy, Roman law as it is called, is something you can all be aware of.

Roman rule spread far and wide. Let me give you just a bit of an idea of how far it spread. If this here is Spain, more or less [drawing on the board], this would be Italy. There we have Greece, the Black Sea. Then a lot of small islands. Asia Minor is coming across from here, and over there, more or less in the area I'll mark for you, was the small country called Palestine, with Jerusalem, Nazareth and so on.

Roman rule extended to all these countries. The Romans had gained dominion over all these countries. And so it was a rule that spread far and wide! Rome is about there, of course. Now all government business and so on would be in Rome, a long way away from Palestine of which people in Rome knew extremely little in those days. And for about a hundred years after the events connected with Christ Jesus in Palestine writers in Rome never mentioned them at all. It was only about a hundred years later that people in Rome became aware of what had happened in Palestine. And the way people looked at it in Rome was not much more than just to say: 'Ah well, some unknown person was crucified in

Palestine.' To be crucified was more or less the same in those days as being hanged in later times. The affair therefore attracted no particular attention. It was only when those hundred years had passed and Roman rule grew more and more tyrannical, and also more and more luxurious, it emerged that in the meantime, whilst the people of Rome lived their life of luxury, Christianity had spread here [pointing to the board] little by little, and the first thing people noticed in Rome was actually the Christians. What happened to the Christians in Rome was that at first people simply would not tolerate them. If you were a Christian, you were very much persecuted in Rome. And now I must tell you why the Christians were persecuted in Rome, otherwise you would of course be quite unable to understand the way of thinking which in those times led people to say that over yonder, in Palestine, a god had died. There you need to understand the way people thought in the world in those times.

You see, for a Roman in the first Christian century, a time, therefore, when one would have said it was the year — people actually did not say it was that year, for they used the Roman calendar then — but if our calendar had already been in use they would have said it was the year 1, or 10, or, if you like, 50 — so if you had asked a Roman 'Who is God?' at that time, he would have said: 'Augustus', or 'Tiberius'. Just as if you were to ask a Chinese today [1923] 'Who is God?', he'd point to the Emperor of China. You have to understand, therefore, that in those days the Romans saw their ruler, the man who governed them, to be their God as well. And the first thing the Romans noticed about the Christians, when they first took note of them, was that the Christians did not believe that a human being here on earth could be a general god. The Romans only knew that someone sitting on the throne, someone who was a mighty ruler, was their god; he was the most sublime and had to be venerated. The Romans did indeed accord their rulers a kind of veneration.

Yes, that is how it was all over the world in those days. Over yonder in the Orient, where the great realms once were—the Persian, Assyrian, Babylonian realms and so on in earlier times—the ruler would always also be the god. 'God' meant simply the one to whom you turned when you were in need of anything. He was the most highly placed. People saw him as a helper. He did not always act as a helper, but people saw him as such.

Let me remind you that you probably also know the way the word 'god' is used in your language. When children are baptized, people have to be their sponsors or godparents. In some areas, I think also here in Switzerland, the sponsors are called 'godfather' and 'godmother'. [The German dialect words are similar to the English ones. Tr.] It means that the sponsors are expected to help the child. This is the same meaning of 'god'. And the god was thus the sponsor for all the world. The name of the German writer Goethe also comes from this.

And the first things people heard about the Christians was that they did not believe that a human being could be a general god on earth. It was something the Romans found unbelievable. Dreadful people who will not accept the emperor as a god! They are dangerous, these people! And the Christians on their part referred to the words: 'Pay the Caesar what is due to the Caesar and pay to God what is due to God.' You can see from those words spoken by Jesus that Caesar and God were separate issues. God is the invisible. God is something which does not dwell in a visible human being on earth. This is what the Christians would say. And that was the big difference between the Romans and Christians. The result was that the Romans considered the Christians to be the most dangerous people in the whole world, people who undermined the power of the state, for they would not offer sacrifices to the emperor in the temple. People would then offer sacrifices to the emperor in the temples. The Christians offered sacrifices to a god who had died in Palestine and could not be seen anywhere. This was something the Romans were unable to grasp.

The early Christians therefore had to hold their offering services below ground, under the earth. And the underground passages they dug, where they buried their dead and made their offerings, are called catacombs. Such catacombs spread far and wide underground in Rome, and in Italy altogether, like small cities. This is where the early Christians held their offering services in the early centuries, whilst the Romans had circuses, vast circuses, above ground. And one of their favourite entertainments in those circuses was to tie people they despised to a stake in some way, to a pillar, cover them with pitch and set fire to them, so that they were burned alive. And people would look at this in their circuses just as people today look at bull fights. It was quite the usual thing in those days.

Now think of this picture. Up above the wild Romans in their circuses, covering people with pitch, tying them to pillars and burning them alive. This was something they enjoyed watching. And below were the Christians, holding their services in the catacombs. The difference, gentlemen, between above and below ground was so great you cannot think of any that would be greater. This is something we have to consider.

It is true, of course, that terrible things were also done by the Inquisition in medieval times. But the Christians never behaved in quite the terrible way the Romans did when their empire was at its height. This is something to be remembered. It is true.

So the first thing you would hear in Rome was: 'The Christians refuse to accept a visible god.' Well, it gradually

became more widely known what was really meant by this
Christ Jesus — I have told you something about this before. I
told you, for example, that there were really two Jesus
boys — Jesus was a common name in Palestine, and many
people were called by it, just like Seppl or Michel today.
One of them died young. They were playmates, we might
say, extraordinarily able, gifted children.

Now you see the story you all know from the Bible about
12-year-old Jesus teaching the scholars in the temple[56] is
based on absolute truth. Now it would not be right for you
to say: 'Yes, but if a 12-year-old boy were to come to the
university today the academic staff would not hold him in
great respect.' One simply cannot compare the teaching of
today with the way it was then. You really should not think
I am being either conservative or reactionary here; I have to
give you the facts as they are.

You know, we do of course have to send our children to
school today. And gifted children in particular learn a great
deal there that does not suit them at all. One should put
things in such a way — and that is what we do in our Waldorf school — that they suit the children. But in general
children are learning a great deal that does not suit them at
all. Adults are of course much better at these things which
do not suit the children at all. But, gentlemen, people fail to
realize today what is taken away from the children when
they learn to read and write in the way they do today.

If you know how to listen to them, children will tell you
extraordinarily interesting things. They have brought these
with them from their life in the spirit before they came
down to earth. And this one Jesus child brought extraordinarily much with him. And as the two Jesus boys were
playmates they would basically always both know the same
things. One of them then died. And the Gospels speak of
only one Jesus child because that was more what people
wanted to hear. But this does not help us to understand the

Gospels. If you read the Gospel of Matthew today and the Gospel of Luke, they do not agree. The whole genealogy of Jesus in the Gospel of Matthew is different from that given in the Gospel of Luke. Why? Well, because these things really refer to two Jesus boys.

As I told you, I have truly spent years on considering this matter from the spiritual point of view. I have found that there were two Jesus children, and the Jesus boy in Matthew's Gospel was a different child from the one in Luke's Gospel.

One of them died in his twelfth year, while the other remained behind. And where the Gospel says: 'Jesus gained in wisdom, spirit and power', this refers only to the one.

You see, I had discovered the fact that there were two Jesus children long before that. One did not know if there was any historical record of there being two Jesus children. And then one day we saw a painting in northern Italy.[57] It shows the scene in the temple where Jesus taught the scripture experts. And oddly enough, there you have this second Jesus child. He is walking off. One who teaches, and the other one who is walking off—that is not the usual Jesus child—we know him! So the painting shows two Jesus children. We are thus able to say that in some centuries people still knew that a second Jesus child existed. He went away. It was only when I had discovered this fact that I knew that this second Jesus was shown in the painting. So you see, gentlemen, that this was known for centuries. But the Church would never let such things, which are in accord with the truth, raise their head.

Now, as I told you, there simply are some things in human life where illumination comes, as we say. People won't accept this, of course. But you see, one can indeed speak of such instances of illumination, for they simply do happen. Let me give you an example that was given to me by a member only yesterday. I could give you hundreds of examples, but let me tell you this, the latest one. Mr Pfeiffer—I hope I have your permission?

Kekulé[58] was a renowned chemist, a proper scientist who wrote many books on chemistry. Two discoveries he made are very important. I need not go into them here, for that would take hours and it is not what matters to us. These two important aspects of chemistry have to do with the nature of the smallest particles that make up substances such as benzene. Kekulé's views on this play an extraordinarily important role in chemistry. Anyone who knows about chemistry knows that everyone is talking of Kekulé's theories.

But how did Kekulé himself experience this? He told of an occasion when he was in London, living quite a long way outside the city—he had not yet developed his theories then—and how he always had to take a bus to the other end of London at night. He would visit a friend in the evenings, and he then always had to go such a long way because he spent the night there. One day he was on his way home, having talked for a long time about chemical things with this friend, who was also a chemist. He was going home and was sitting on the top deck of the bus, on the outside. He was dozing off, beginning to fall asleep. And as he was about to fall asleep on the bus he dreamt: There's one atom, there's another, there a third atom; and there are little atoms, and they are held together by the big ones [drawing on the board]. He dreamt of the way matter is made up. He dreamt all this up on top of the bus. He made careful notes of it as soon as he got home. This was one of his theories. You see, it came to him in a dream. It was given to him, a completely materialistic theory.

His second theory is called the benzene theory. He dreamt it at another time, not in London this time, but when he had dozed off somewhere else.[59]

Well, gentlemen, you see, a completely materialistic

chemist had to confess that he did not make his discoveries by thinking things through but was given illumination in a dream. All of it was truly given.

Now I'd like to know why people object when one says that the Jesus who remained behind changed greatly in this thirtieth year. Kekulé did not, of course, immediately become a different person, for the inspiration given to him had been a minor one. But knowledge of the whole world entered into Jesus when he was 30 years old. This was perfectly possible in earlier times, and similar things can still happen today. So you just have to consider that Jesus of Nazareth was illuminated in his thirtieth year with every-thing that is called 'the Christ'. The Christ entered into him, just as the benzene theory entered into Kekulé. He then became a completely different person. And people who understood something of this said: 'The Romans have a god on the throne.' 'The god on the throne,' they would say, 'has come into being through the ordinary powers of the earth.' Such gods on thrones do not normally have illumination; at least not as a rule, you know; they did not receive such illumination at the age of 30.

Now the Christians said: 'Our God has not been put there by human beings; he has been put there by the powers of the universe themselves.'

They also had to say something else, however. You see, the things they said about Jesus at the time were not as indefinite as the things I am telling you now. I have to tell it to you slowly, bit by bit, you see, and this makes it all rather indefinite to begin with. It was more definite then in the following way. You see, today, we have universities so that individual people may grow clever in the way people are considered clever today. Having spent a long time being made clever at a grammar school or secondary school, people go to university. There their cleverness is given its final polish. But you'll not always find that people have become different people at university; they have only learnt things in a superficial way.

That was not the way it was in earlier times. In earlier times people made no difference between churches, theatres and schools. It was all one, and they called it 'the mysteries'. These were the places where people were taught then. And the most important thing they were taught in the mysteries was 'knowledge of the sun', as it was called.

You see, when we talked about scientific matters, I always told you that the sun influences everything that happens on earth. Plants do not just grow because they are pushed up out of the soil, but because the sun brings them forth. Sun power is in all of us, just as there is earth power. And I told you that this sun power is not just a dead force, but a living power, full of wisdom. I gave you many examples. You were able to see that the things that happen among animals happen in a way that is full of wisdom, intelligent, sensible. Yes, if you look up to the sun, it is a sphere of gas, scientists will say. Well, gentlemen, that is just about as clever as if we could all of us get on a large plane — we can't do it, of course, but let us assume we could, the way Jules Verne has written about it — and go up to the moon, looking for something to do on the moon. And I'd then say to you: 'Look, gentlemen, down there is the earth. The earth is a body, and there is nothing else on it.' You would not believe me, gentlemen, because you'll have travelled up to the moon with me. You would believe that there are people on the earth, after all. People, who have souls, are on the earth.

But that is exactly what scientists do when it comes to the sun today. They sit here on the earth, look up at the sun and say: 'There is nothing up there but burning gas.' But that is downright nonsense. The sun is inhabited, though perhaps not by the kind of people you can see with your eyes.

In the ancient mysteries, people were mainly given this

knowledge of the sun. And because of this, they were called 'sun scholars'. People would say: 'Up there, on the sun, are the powers, the powers of spring, the powers of the sun, the principle which draws everything forth from the earth.' And someone who had learned those secrets of the sun would then be called a sun scholar, and later, when he was fully taught, a sun master. And the knowledge that came suddenly to Jesus of Nazareth in his thirtieth year was this sun wisdom. This sun wisdom had come upon him. Now you have probably seen plants which are a good green colour in the soil, robust plants, go quite white and powerless if they are kept below ground, in a cellar. The sun's power does not enter into them there. In a mystic, spiritual sense, this sun power entered into Jesus. And the people who understood what had happened said: 'Now the Christ has entered into Jesus.'

You see, now this strange thing happened. The Jews, who then lived mainly here, in Palestine [pointing to the blackboard], had long since heard through their prophets that it would have to happen one day that the earth could be taught out of cosmic space itself. But you can be quite sure, if someone somewhere were to write a play like *William Tell* today, the way Schiller has written it, and it were to be performed on stage, people would say: 'That's baloney, it's quite terrible.' They would not accept it. The play was only accepted by a few people at first, people who knew Schiller. Then it got more widely known. That's the way it is in our society, and always has been, that the majority of people like to take their lead from others. And the Jews, too, took their lead from others and when the event happened, and they were no longer guided by the mysteries but someone came instead who had this sun wisdom, they said: 'Well, really. Here's someone who says everything he says is true.' You know what people do to someone who speaks a truth that has not yet got known among the populace. It was a great truth and great wisdom which Jesus of Nazareth, in whom the Christ now lived, had to tell. Well, they crucified him. And he did indeed go through death.

This now brings me to the question as it was put to me. You see, gentlemen, today's enlightened theologians are perhaps even worse, in most cases, than the unenlightened ones. Unenlightened theologians say: 'Well, they put the Christ in his tomb, and after three days he rose again, flesh and blood, as he had been.' Well, enlightened people would of course say: 'We don't believe that, for no one returns from the grave.' But, I'd say, they do at least have something they are able to profess. It may be debatable, but it is something they are able to profess.

But what do enlightened theologians say? You see, one of the most enlightened theologians, a man who is widely known and often spoken of, is Adolf von Harnack.[60] And what does he say about the resurrection? You see, Mr Harnack says: 'We cannot tell what happened there on the third day in the Garden at Gethsemane.' This, then, is what an enlightened theologian says: 'We cannot tell what happened there on the third day in the Garden at Gethsemane. Many people did gradually come to believe that the Christ was risen there. That is belief in the Easter story, and we assume that one should hold to this belief.'

You see, I once put this question at the Giordano Bruno Association in Berlin — it was a long time ago now. The chairman was a learned gentleman who thought he knew a great deal about these things. He said: 'Surely Harnack cannot have said that, for where would we be if Harnack were to say that we should not believe in what has really happened but only in what people think about it.' That would be like the story of the robe at Trier[61] where people said: 'Well, we don't know if this is the robe that the Christ actually wore, but so many people believed this, and so we believe it as well.' That is what a Protestant said about

Catholic faith in the robe at Trier. Another example are the bones of St Anthony. When they were carefully examined they turned out to be calves' bones. But the people who believed in them did not let this worry them; they said it did not matter if it was true or not but only that people believed it.

It is not that it does not matter, however, but it matters what actually happened. The story is really told in a wonderful way in the Bible, but people do not pay attention to the way it is told. The Bible does not say: such and such a thing happened. It always says: this is what people saw, really saw. This is what the Bible tells.

So the story is that the women went out there and it tells us what they saw at the tomb. You may of course take it to be sophistry, if you like! We are told that the Christ came to the disciples at Emmaus, and so on; that the Christ was seen. This is what the Bible tells us.

Now you'll remember I told you that human beings do not only have this material, physical body which is laid in the grave, but they also have the ether body, astral body and I. I described this to you very exactly. And the physical body of Jesus of Nazareth was indeed put in a tomb. I have considered this question a great deal, and it is extraordinarily significant that the Bible itself tells us that an earthquake happened. Such an earthquake did happen. It made a cleft, and the body was taken up into the earth, so that it truly was no longer there. And the disciples did not see this physical body but the ether body, the supersensible body. The women and the disciples saw the Christ in the ether body, no longer Jesus of Nazareth but the Christ, the transformed inner human being.

Now you have to imagine that what happened there was something extraordinarily grand for the disciples. You just have to imagine that one of you, someone with whom you have come to be good friends, is taken away from you to be crucified, or hanged, as it would be today. You are closely connected with this person — this creates a state of mind. And such a state of mind made the disciples positively clairvoyant for these things. And in those early days they truly saw the Christ over and over again, more often than the Bible tells us. But it was the supersensible Christ.

And you see, if you read the epistles of Paul, you read there of the famous event at Damascus which came to Paul. Near Damascus he went into a kind of sleep state and the Christ appeared to him in the clouds. And now consider how Paul told the story. He once said: 'They cannot take away my faith in the Christ, for like the other apostles I have seen the Christ.'

Paul therefore did not say that the other apostles had seen the Christ in a physical body; for then he would have to say that he, too, had seen the Christ in a physical body. He emphatically said that he had seen the Christ in the clouds, and that is the supersensible Christ. In saying that he and the other apostles had seen the Christ, he was indicating that the other apostles saw the Christ in his supersensible body, just as he did. And then, you know, people say this is contradicted by the fact that Thomas had to put his hands on the wounds of the Christ. All this is meant to say, however, is that the Christ was there, and the experience of his presence was so powerful that Thomas himself was able to believe firmly that he had touched him. Everything therefore had to do with the supersensible Christ.

Now you know, the wounds were something that touched the hearts of the disciples, and especially the apostles, most deeply. This would not show itself so clearly if the Gospels did not say that the wounds could be touched. Why the wounds, exactly? Why not put his hands on the face or something else? There he would also have felt that there was something there. But he put his finger on the wounds because the wounds made a particular impression, and it did indeed depend on higher vision what the disciple actually became aware of in the Christ.

We may thus say that for 40 days in succession the disciples knew clearly that the Christ was still there.

And this gave rise to the Christian teaching — the original Christian teaching, which is connected with the things I told you last Monday — it gave rise to the Christians saying: 'When the Christ was buried, only the dead body was in the tomb, and it disappeared, of course. The Christ revealed the immortal aspect to us in himself; he went about for 40 days in his immortal aspect. We have seen him. And he even appeared to Paul at a much later time. He is therefore always present.'

And so we can say, even today: 'He is always present.' The disciples no longer saw him after 40 days because their vision lost its power. They then said: 'Now he has gone away from us.' The ascension was an event that did, of course, make the disciples feel very sad. They said: 'Although he died, although his enemies crucified him, he was still among us for 40 days. Now he is no longer among us. Now he has gone back again into the wide expanse of the cosmos.'

And they truly felt sad then. Not the usual kind of sadness, but a profound sadness. And the ten days of which we then read, those ten days were a time when the disciples and apostles turned inwards, looking deep into their hearts, using their inner strength to think of all the things the Christ had said to them. Those ten days were enough for them to be able to say afterwards: 'Yes, we, too, are able to know all this. This wisdom' — they said to themselves under that powerful impression — 'this wisdom is also in us.' And now, after ten days, they felt strong enough also to teach the wisdom to others. The tongues of fire — that is an image of this — came down on to their heads. That was Pentecost, the Pentecost thought, the tongues of fire. In their great sadness, having thought about everything, not being able to see the Christ any more, had made them turn inwards to such effect that they themselves were then able to teach. And we read the beautiful words that they then began to 'speak in all tongues'. But here we have to understand a little how people put things in earlier times. You should not think, of course, that the apostles started to speak Chinese or Japanese, or even German. What is meant, in the way of saying things they had in those times, is that because of everything they had had in their thoughts in the ten days between the ascension and Pentecost they had grown tolerant. Now they no longer saw differences between religions but spoke of one religion for all human beings. This is what is meant by saying they were able to speak in all tongues; they spoke of one religion for all humanity.

And that is the best of all thoughts for Pentecost—one religion for all humanity. You see, the greatest harm has always come to humanity from fanaticism in religious things, being exclusive in religion, having Christianity and Buddhism and Judaism and all kinds of things. Why is it that there are so many religions? It is because these religions are earth religions, real earth religions.

What do I mean when I say earth religions? Well, you see, there was a time—it is 1923 now—if we go back, for example, to the time when Christ Jesus lived in Palestine, as I have told you, which would be the turning-point of time. Now let us go further back, let us say to the year 3500 before Christ Jesus, to antiquity. At that time, 3000 or 3500 years before Christ, people in Egypt would speak of their god, but they would use the old terms. They would call him Ra, for instance. They would speak of their god, but they would say: 'The god is in the city of Thebes,' for instance, and in the city of Thebes stood a building that had been created with great art, a tomb-like structure. The god lived in there.

That was the earliest way of venerating one's god, by saying he was in a particular place.

Well, gentlemen, someone living here where we live today in those early times would probably not have said: 'The god is in Thebes.' Not only would they never have got to that place in those times, but they would not have known anything about it. They really did not know about Thebes. So the people who were down here in Egypt, where the Nile flows, they would say: 'The god lives in Thebes.' And the people who were here, in our part of the world, also had such local gods. There was a local god in Alsace once, for example, or in Münster. People therefore venerated God in a particular place. And it is because of this that we have different religions — the religion of Thebes, the religion of Münster, the religion of Alsace. There the religions got divided up.

And later, when people had moved around more on earth, they could no longer think of God in a particular place, for then they would have contradicted themselves. They had moved to another place, and then they no longer took the place for the god but the individual who led them. And that is how emperors and princes gradually came to be seen as gods. The prince of one nation would be the emperor. Many princes came into existence.

You see, they still had something of this religion in Rome, for the Romans still venerated their emperor as their god.

But what, then, was Christianity? Christianity had nothing of all this. The divine spirit we should venerate is not in a particular place on earth but is connected with the power of the sun, the living nature of the sun which the Christ has taken into himself. And the sun is truly for the whole of humanity. No one in Europe can say, when the sun is shining on his head, that this is a different sun from the one that is there for the Egyptians, or the Chinese, or the Australians. Anyone who truly accepts that the Christ power comes from the sun has to accept the general religion that is for all humanity.

It was the general religion for all humanity, even if people did not always understand this. And the disciples realized very well that the sun religion had come. The way it is put is to say that they were able to speak in all tongues. They were able to speak of a religion of reconciliation, of tolerance for all humanity. That is the Pentecost idea. But, as you know, the Pentecost idea has not yet come to fulfilment today. And it must come to fulfilment. It must be truly understood that the Christ has brought something to this earth that does not depend on any form of teaching at all but is based on a fact.

When European missionaries go to an Indian or a Chinese person today, they ask him to believe what people in Rome say of the Christ. The Indians or the Chinese cannot agree to this, for it is something that has developed in the European situation. But if one were to put it the way I have put it to you today, it could be understood everywhere on earth. For the Pentecost idea is for the whole of humanity.

I have tried now to present the ascension idea to you, as we should take it, and the Pentecost idea. This is what the gentleman who wrote down the question wanted to know. I think it is also very appropriate, for today is the day before Ascension, and Pentecost will follow in ten days' time. I am very glad that I was able to speak about this.

Now I have to go to Norway. I'll ask them to tell you when our next talk will be. Goodbye for now!

Translator's note

A list is given below of foreign words and their rough-and-ready pronunciation for those who feel they'd like to get it more or less right.

Burle	boorle
Virchow	virko
Jena	yaina
Büttner	bittner
Baden	barden
Hohenzollern	ho hen tsollan
Müller	miller
Hauer	how a
Erbsmehl	airps male
Aare	ah re
Reuss	royce
Seppl	scepl
Michel	me chl (short e, ch like the h in human)
Pfeiffer	pfifer
Kekulé	cake oolay
Münster	minster
Boos	boce

Notes

Text source. The lectures were taken down by Helene Finkh (1883–1960), a professional stenographer, and written out in cleartext by her. The original shorthand records were completely reviewed for the 2nd (1980) German edition, on which this translation is based, and a new cleartext produced. Changes in the text compared to earlier German editions would be due to this.

Original blackboard drawings are in vol. XXVI of *Wandtafelzeichnungen zum Vortragswerk*, Dornach: Rudolf Steiner Verlag 1994.

GA = *Gesamtausgabe* (German edition of the collected works of Rudolf Steiner).

1 Details of this lecture have not yet been traced.
2 See *The Human Being in Body, Soul and Spirit; Early Conditions of the Earth* (GA 347), talks of 20, 23, 27 & 30 September 1922, tr. J. Reuter, New York: Anthroposophic Press 1989.
3 A large sloth, now extinct, from the Megatheriidae family. Existed from the Miocene to the Pleistocene periods of earth history.
4 Dornach lies in the Jura mountain range in Switzerland, and these are limestone.
5 Reference to Calcium Supplement, produced according to suggestions made by Rudolf Steiner by the Weleda company. See also Steiner, R., *Conferences with Rudolf Steiner* (GA 300 c), conference of 14 February 1923, AWSNA Publications.
6 Allopathy is a term introduced by Hahnemann in 1842, to mark the opposite of homoeopathy. It means 'different pathology', i.e. treating a medical problem by introducing one of a different kind, whereas homoeopathy means treating it with a substance that will produce the same kind of symptoms. The matter of dosage is secondary to both, and both material and dilute doses may be used in either, but in

popular language 'homoeopathic' has come to mean 'in small doses'. (Translator)

7   Virchow, Rudolf (1821–1902), German pathologist, a founder of cellular pathology.

8   *Health and Illness* (GA 348), vols 1 and 2 (esp. vol. 2), tr. M. St Goar, New York: Anthroposophic Press 1981 and 1983.

9   Rudolf Steiner had also spoken about the connections between red and blue, blood and nerve, in colour therapy in a lecture given on 5 April 1920, published in *Spiritual Science and Medicine* (GA 312), tr. not known, London: Rudolf Steiner Publishing Co. 1948.

10   Newton, Isaac (1642–1727), English mathematician and natural philosopher. See Steiner, R., *Goethean Science* (GA 1c), tr. W. Lindemann, Spring Valley: Mercury Press 1988.

11   Reference to the town of Basel, where the carnival is held on a different date from elsewhere. People living there might therefore celebrate two carnivals.

12   Vegetable paints were produced in a specially set up laboratory, using methods suggested by Rudolf Steiner, and used for the paintings in the two domes of the First Goetheanum. In the 1930s, the Anthea Institute of Vegetable Paint Research in Dornach produced and sold 16 colours and a medium. In recent years, vegetable paints have been produced again at the Vegetable Paint Workshop at the Goetheanum.

13   Büttner, Christian William, naturalist and linguist, professor in Göttingen, court counsellor living in Jena, had lent his optical instruments to Goethe. Goethe told the story in the chapter 'author's confession' in *Materialien zur Geschichte der Farblehre* (material relating to the history of the theory of colour) (eighteenth century) in vol. 4, section 2 of Naturwissenschaftliche Schriften in Kürschner's National-Litteratur.

14   It has to be remembered that the things said about the rainbow, which in themselves were only brief indications, were taken down imperfectly in shorthand, leaving gaps. In Goethe's theory of colour edited by Rudolf Steiner and

published as part of Kürschner's National-Litteratur in 1897, the comment on Goethe's statement concerning the rainbow reads: 'The rainbow is a case of refraction, perhaps the most complex of all, with reflection involved as well. The light must pass through the drop, i.e. it is broken (refraction), but must then come back to us who are between the sun and the drop, i.e. it must be reflected.' Band V, S. 329 ff. in the German edition.

15 Dante Alighieri (1265–1321).

16 Nicolas Copernicus (1473–1543), canon of Frauenburg Cathedral, founder of modern astronomy.

17 Lavoisier, Antoine Laurent (1743–94), French chemist.

18 Archimedes (*c.* 287–212 BC), Greek mathematician, physicist and inventor.

19 Steiner, R., *Knowledge of the Higher Worlds, How is it Achieved?* (GA 10), tr. D.S. Osmond, C. Davy, London: Rudolf Steiner Press 1976. Also available as *How to Know Higher Worlds. A Modern Path of Initiation*, tr. C. Bamford, Hudson: Anthroposophic Press 1994.

20 Du Bois-Reymond, Emil (1818–86), physiologist in Berlin. His *Ignorabimus* speech had the title 'On the limits to our knowledge of nature', and was given at the second general session of the 45th German Naturalists and Medical Conference on 14 August 1872 in Leipzig.

21 Literally: 'Berlin University, placed opposite to the royal palace, is the academic "sovereign's own regiment" of the House of Hohenzollern.' Du Bois-Reymond in an academic address given on 3 August 1870.

22 See note 19.

23 The dogma of pre-existence was rejected for the followers of Origen at a synod held in Constantinople in 543 and for the Priscillianists at a synod held in Braga in 561.

24 Probably Wilhelm Foerster (1823–1921).

25 Anzengruber, Ludwig (1839–89), Austrian writer, in his play *Ein Faustschlag* (1878), Act 3, Scene 6, Kammauf's actual words: 'for ... as true as God ... I am an atheist!'

26 It has not so far been possible to identify the book.

27 See note 19.
28 Richter, Johann Paul Friedrich (1763–1825), pseudonym Jean Paul, German novelist. In his *Levana*, a work on education, he wrote in the preface to the first edition on 2 May 1806: 'The first volume goes more fully into the bud period of a child than the second and third do into the flowering period. In the first, attention and concern focuses on what we may call the academic three-year course after which the door to the soul, speech, finally opens.' And in his sixth fragment, chapter 4, paragraph 122: 'The fruits of a good upbringing in the first three years (a higher-ranking three-year course than the academic one) you cannot harvest whilst you are sowing ... but after some years riches in abundance will grow to surprise and reward you.'
29 Steiner, R., *Occult Science. An Outline* (GA 13), tr. G. & M. Adams, rev. London: Rudolf Steiner Press 1971.
30 Tagore, Sir Rabindranath (1861–1941), Indian poet and philosopher, born in Calcutta. His *Reminiscences* had just appeared in German translation at the time.
31 Lessing, Gotthold Ephraim (1729–81), German writer.
32 Mehring, Franz (1846–1919), German left-wing writer, one of the founders of the German Communist Party. Wrote historical studies of the workers' movement.
33 Crookes, Sir William (1832–1919), OM, born in London, chemistry lecturer at Science College, Chester.
34 *Observations upon the Prophecies of Daniel and the Apocalypse of St John*, published posthumously, London 1733.
35 Cocaine, a white alkaloid extracted from the leaves of the South American coca shrub (Bolivian leaf from *Erythroxylon coca* or Peruvian leaf from *E. truxillense*).
36 It has not so far been possible to trace this newpaper item.
37 Hauer, J.W., *Werden und Wesen der Anthroposophie* (Origins and nature of anthroposophy), Stuttgart 1922.
38 Venus's fly-trap (*Dionaea muscipula*), member of the sundew family (*Drosera*). See Darwin on insect-eating plants, in his collected works.
39 Plato (*c.* 427–347 BC), Athenian philosopher. The passage

about Solon, the Athenian lawgiver, is in the *Timaeus* dialogues, translated as *Plato's Cosmology* by F.M. Cornford in 1937.

40 Julian, Flavius Claudius Julianus, 'the Apostate' (*c*. 331–63). Concerning the triple sun, see also the lecture Rudolf Steiner gave in London on 24 April 1922 (in GA 211), *Man's Life on Earth and in the Spiritual Worlds*, tr. G. & M. Adams. London: Anthroposophical Publishing Co. 1952.

41 Matthew 3:17.

42 Goethe, 'Zahme Xenien' VI, 32, in collected poetic works (in German).

43 See Steiner, R., *Spiritual Guidance of the Individual and Humanity* (GA 15), tr. S. Desch, New York: Anthroposophic Press 1992.

44 Described by Hella Krause-Zimmer in her book *Die zwei Jesusknaben in der bildenden Kunst*, S. 157 ff. and 159 ff., Stuttgart 1997.

45 Matthew 3:16.

46 Steiner, R., *Christianity as Mystical Fact* (GA 8), tr. A. Welburn, Hudson: Anthroposophic Press 1997.

47 Carbo Betulae, Weleda Co.

48 Fresh lily of the valley flowers are expressed and processed by special methods.

49 Former name of phenacetin.

50 *The Representative of Man Between Lucifer and Ahriman*, at the Goetheanum in Dornach.

51 D.L. Johannes Frohnmeyer (1850–1921). The passage in question from *Die theosophische Bewegung, ihre Geschichte, Darstellung und Beurteilung;* S. 107, Stuttgart 1920, reads: 'A 9-metre-high statue of the ideal human being is currently being carved in Dornach, with 'luciferic' traits in its upper and animal characteristics in its lower parts' (omitted from the 2nd edition). Frohnmeyer took this information from an article written by pastor Heinrich Nidecker-Roos (*Christlicher Volksbote aus Basel* 1920; 88: 23: 179 f., 9 June 1920) without checking it, and without giving the source, as if this was something he had established himself, rather than go to

Dornach from nearby Basel and look at the sculpture himself. See also lectures given on 16 January and 6 February 1921, in GA 203 S. 76 ff. and 193 ff. (not available in English).

52   Boos, Roman (1889–1952), lawyer and social scientist, active representative of anthroposophy, leading figure in the threefold movement in Switzerland.

53   In a publication called *Die Hetze gegen das Goetheanum*, S. 106, Dornach 1920, which included a lecture by Rudolf Steiner on the truth about anthroposophy and defending it against untruthfulness, and Dr Boos's article.

54   Letter dated 23 January 1921.

55   Rudolf Steiner suggested using a medicament made from mistletoe grown on poplars to treat cancer of the liver.

56   Luke 2:41–52.

57   Painting by Borgognone in St Ambrogio Church in Milan.

58   Kekulé von Stradonitz, Friedrich August (1829–96), German chemist, professor at Ghent and Bonn Universities.

59   Ehrenfried Pfeiffer gave Rudolf Steiner part of Gustav Schultz's report on the German Chemical Society's celebrations held in Berlin in 1890 in honour of Kekulé's birthday. The two incidents August Kekulé described are given below.

'When I was in London I was staying in Clapham Road, near the Common, for some time. But I would often spend my evenings with my friend Hugo Müller in Islington, which is on the opposite side of that vast city. We would talk about all kinds of things, and most of all about our beloved chemistry. On a beautiful summer's day I was once again taking the last bus through the streets, now empty, of the normally busy cosmopolitan city; outside, on the top of the bus, as ever. I fell into a dream. Then the atoms were dancing before my eyes. I had always seen those tiny entities in motion, in my mind's eye, but had never been able to get a feeling of the way they moved. On that occasion I saw how two would often make a pair, two larger ones would encompass two smaller ones, even larger ones take hold of three or even four of the smallest, with everything in a